IMAGES OF WAR
THE FEW:
PREPARATION FOR THE
BATTLE OF BRITAIN

RARE PHOTOGRAPHS FROM WARTIME ARCHIVES

PHILIP KAPLAN

First printed in Great Britain in 2014 by
Pen & Sword Aviation
an imprint of
Pen & Sword Books Ltd.
47 Church Street
Barnsley,
South Yorkshire
S70 2AS

A CIP record for this book is available from the British Library.

ISBN 978 1 78346 287 2

Printed and bound in England
By CPI Group (UK) Ltd. Croydon, CR0 4YY

Pen & Sword Books Ltd incorporates the Imprints of Pen & Sword Aviation, Pen & Sword Family History, Pen & Sword Maritime, Pen & Sword Military, Pen & Sword Discovery, Wharncliffe Local History, Wharncliffe True Crime, Wharncliffe Transport, Pen & Sword Select, Pen & Sword Military Classics, Leo Cooper, The Praetorian Press, Remember When, Seaforth Publishing and Frontline Publishing.

For a complete list of Pen & Sword titles please contact Pen & Sword Books Limited
47 Church Street, Barnsley, South Yorkshire, S70 2AS, England

E-mail: enquiries@pen-and-sword.co.uk
Website: www.pen-and-sword.co.uk

Contents

The author is grateful to Margaret Mayhew, whose generous help, suggestions, ideas and assistance were invaluable. Special thanks to the many Battle of Britain participants for their kind contributions and assistance. A special thank you too, to the following people for providing additional photos, information, interviews, gifts and loans of personal memorabilia, as well as other forms of assistance: Monique Agazarian, Tad Andersz, J.A. Baker, Malcolm Bates, RAF Bentley Priory, Tony Bianchi, Harold Bird-Wilson, Kazimierz Budzik, C.J. Bunney, John Burgess, Richard Bye, Geoffrey Charters, Pat Collier, Richard Collier for his superb text, Jack Currie, Alan C. Deere, R.F.T. Doe, Neville Duke, Gary Eastman, Richard Erven, Gilly Fielder, Bob Fisher, Brian Forbes, Christopher Foxley-Norris, Dave Glaser, Ella Freire, Joan Goodman, Barry Gregory, Stephen Grey, Jonathan Grimwood, Tony Iacono, Lynn Johnson, Claire and Joe Kaplan, Neal Kaplan, Brian Kingcome, Bud Knapp, Tadeusz Krzystek, Edith Kup, Reg Mack, Eric Marsden, Mike Mathews, Tilly McMaster, Edward R. Murrow, Lynn Newmark, John Newth, Michael O'Leary, Geoffrey Page, Pauline Page, Keith Park, Horst Petzschler, Alan Reeves, Edward Reeves, R.A. Reiss, Mark Ritchie, Andy Saunders, William L. Shirer, Mary Smith, San Diego Aerospace Museum, Tangmere Military Aviation Museum, Peter Townsend, Chris von Glahn, Ray Wagner, and Frank Wootton, The Bundesarchiv, The Imperial War Museum, The U.S. National Archives and Records Administration, The Royal Air Force Museum.
Reaonable efforts have beenmade to trace the copyright holders to use their material. The author apologizes for any omissions. All reasonable efforts will be made to correct such omissions in future editions of this work.

The Unease

The key word of the age was 'appeasement'. It was whispered through the chancellories and conference chambers of the nineteen-thirties as insidiously as the pop tunes of the day permeated the lives of the people: *'Top Hat'*, *'Smoke Gets In Your Eyes'*, *'Love In Bloom'*. It signified, in essence, a tacit acceptance of naked aggression: that Adolf Hitler, Führer and Chancellor of the Third Reich, should, at noon on March 7, 1936, send a handful of battalions to occupy the 9,000 square miles of the demilitarized Rhineland in defiance of the 1919 Treaty of Versailles. This was a treaty, which was designed to curb the militarism of Kaiser Wilhelm's time, that still, after seventeen years, rankled in so many German breasts.

Appeasement meant that Benito Mussolini, Italy's *Il Duce* of Fascism, whose goal was a new and glorious Roman Empire, could, with impunity, on October 3, 1935, launch an unprovoked seven-month conquest of the ancient kingdom of Ethiopia. Since the sanctions invoked by the 50-strong League of Nations—another creation of Versailles—stopped short of oil, the Duce's brigandage went unopposed.

Never openly voiced, although silently acknowledged, was the realization that World War Two would involve whoever opposed the dictators in a rain of devastation from the air—and that the air forces of the uneasy allies, Britain and France, were in no shape to counter that threat.

The much vaunted Royal Air Force, formed on April 1, 1918, had soon stood revealed as the nine-day wonder that it was. A total of 184 squadrons operational on Armistice Day had, by early 1920,

below: British Prime Minister Neville Chamberlain; below right: A David Low cartoon of 1940 captioned, *'Ooo! See what that wicked Chamberlain makes me do'.*P

left: A Schneider Trophy race programme from 1931; below: Assembling the wings of the prototype Hawker Hurricane at Kingston, London, in 1935; bottom left: Instructors and students of the London Air Squadron preparing for an afternoon's flying in their Avro Tudor aircraft; bottom right: RAF students and instructors and their DeHavilland Tiger Moth trainers.

whittled down to eighteen—of which only three were based in England. Although 1925 saw the creation of an Auxiliary Air Force, an officers-only Territorial Association of wealthy amateurs, who made up 'the finest flying club in the world', and a Royal Air Force Volunteer Reserve, aimed at raising RAF strength from 29,000 to 90,000 in three years, had barely reached the drawing board stage by June 1935.

Behind this compound of stupidity, cowardice and petty self-interest lay a genuine belief that Hitler and Mussolini, initially seen as bastions of order and stability against the extreme left, were essentially responsible statesmen. And, given enough territory they would, ultimately, prove quite amenable to reason. ("Hitler", Lord Lothian, a prominent appeaser among the Liberal Party's ranks, rationalized the Rhineland seizure, "is doing nothing more than taking over his own back garden.") Conveniently ignored were the truths that the National Socialists had for three years worked as silently as termites in timber, in flagrant defiance of Versailles, to create a standing army of 500,000 men, and a Luftwaffe of almost 2,000 aircraft. For Hitler's freely-avowed aim was *Lebensraum* (living space), a Reich whose frontiers would soon extend beyond all normally accepted frontiers, and ultimately Lebensraum would mean war.

All through the late nineteen-thirties, when the pipe of Stanley Baldwin and the umbrella of his successor, Neville Chamberlain, symbolized security for so many of the British, the RAF were striving to keep pace. On November 6, 1935, five weeks after Mussolini's Ethiopian incursion, the first of designer Sydney Camm's Hawker Hurricane Mark Is, was airborne from Brooklands airfield in Surrey, climbing to 15,000 feet with a top speed of 330 mph. Although 1,000 would be ordered, the first would not reach their destined squadron, No. 111, until well into January 1938. On March 5, 1936, two days before the Rhineland debacle, Reginald Joseph Mitchell's little blue monoplane fighter, already

Vickers manufacturing and assembly photos in the Castle Bromwich Spitfire plant during the Second World War.

known as the Spitfire, soared triumphantly on its own test flight, above the blue waters of the Solent at Eastleigh, Hampshire. An initial 450 would be bespoken from Vickers-Supermarine; it would be August 1938 before 19 Squadron at Duxford traded in their Gloster Gauntlets for the first of these new machines.

Throughout 1936, the landmarks charting the way to the greatest air war in history became increasingly apparent. On July 14, Air Marshal Sir Hugh Caswall Tremenheere Dowding arrived at 'the most singular place on earth', the 166-year-old Bentley Priory, perched on a hilltop at Stanmore, Middlesex, to form the headquarters of the newly-created Fighter Command. A remote and glacial widower, then aged fifty-four, Air Marshal Dowding, invariably known as "Stuffy", faced a task more formidable than any air commander had ever known.

Four months later, the Condor Legion, 370 handpicked fliers, assembled in Seville, bent on abetting General Francisco Franco's Nationalist Armed Forces in their struggle against the Republicans that marked the Spanish Civil War. As Hitler saw it, this was an invaluable proving ground for his new Luftwaffe, and the Führer was right; one up-and-coming ace, Leutnant Adolf Galland, flew 280 missions over the hotly-contested Ebro River. Above all, the campaign was an unparalleled boost to Luftwaffe morale; the tactical successes of the Junkers 87 dive-bombers—the Stukas—conjured up a chilling, if ultimately misleading, picture of twentieth century air power. "The Stukas in Spain," one historian noted, "spread fear far beyond it."

As far, indeed, as Austria, where no voices were raised in protest between February 12 and March 11, 1938, as Adolf Hitler achieved a bloodless *Anschluss* (union) of that country with his Third Reich. As far, on the dark, rainy Friday afternoon of August 5, as Czechoslovakia, when the code word 'Diabolo' brought Fighter Command, for the first time, to a state of war readiness. At Biggin Hill, in Kent, pilots like Pete Brothers and Michael Crossley, and others of No. 32 Squadron, sadly set to work with pots and brushes, disfiguring their gleaming Gloster Gauntlets with drab green and brown camouflage. Out went 32 Squadron's crest, emblazoned on every rudder, a "Hunting horn stringed in a broad white arrow." Alongside them worked the pilots of Squadron Leader Paddy Pritchett's 79 Squadron, silently obliterating their "Salamander salient in flames."

In truth, the alarm was premature. Czechoslovakia's western province, the Sudetenland, with its large German-speaking minority, would, through the complicity of Neville Chamberlain and France's Edouard Daladier, be "given" to Hitler through the mechanism of the September 29 Munich conference, a last-ditch attempt to forestall the Führer marching in on October 1. It was a conference from which the Czechs, from first to last, were ostentatiously excluded. "It is peace in our time," Chamberlain told the cheering crowds at London's Heston airport.

"This is my last territorial demand in Europe," Hitler was to assure Chamberlain and the world, a promise which at least one sceptic begged leave to doubt. "This time it is different," Chamberlain contradicted him, baring his teeth in a complacent smile, "This time he has made his promises to me."

left top and bottom: Final assembly of new Mark IX Spitfire fighters at the Castle Bromwich, Birmingham, Spitfire plant in the Second World War. Castle Bromwich produced more than 11,500 Spitfires and Seafires during the war years.

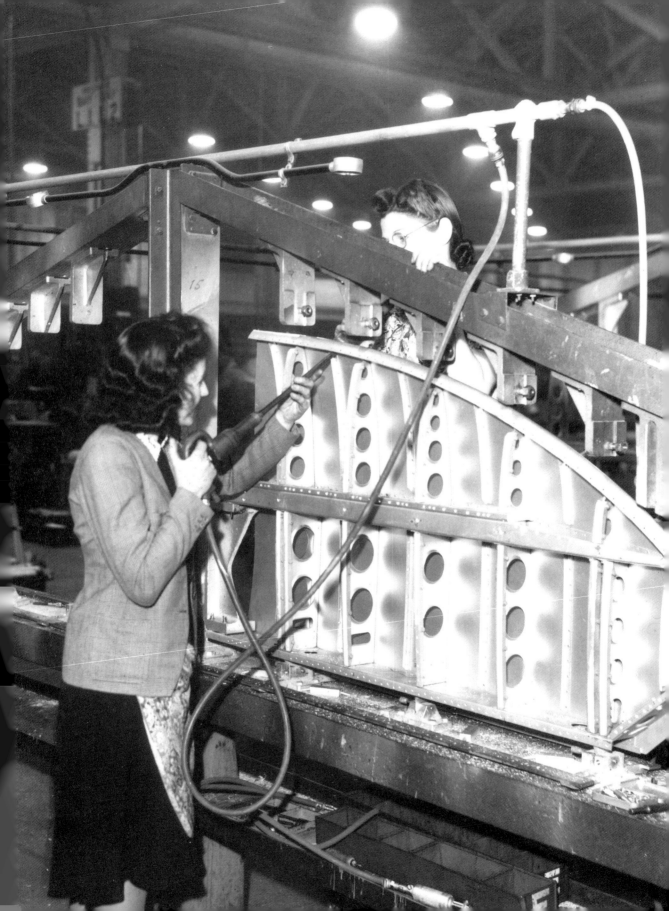

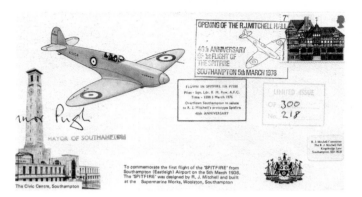

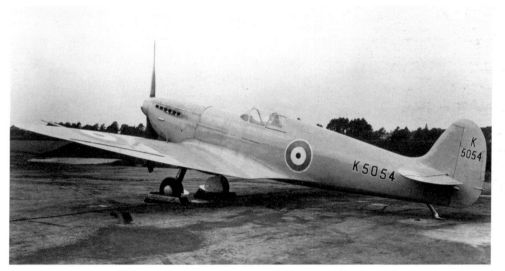

far left: Rivetting a tail assembly for a Spitfire at Castle Bromwich; left: The Spitfire prototype in 1936; at top: Postal commemoratives for the Spitfire; below: The Hawker Hurricane prototype in 1935.

A State of War

The English love their country with a love / Steady and simple, wordless, dignified; I think its sets their patriotism above / All others. We Americans have pride. / We glory in our country's short romance. We boast of it and love it. Frenchmen when / The ultimate menace comes, will die for France / Logically as they lived. But Englishmen Will serve day after day, obey the law, / And do dull tasks that keep a nation strong. Once I remember in London how I saw / Pale shabby people standing in a long line in the twilight and the misty rain / To pay their tax. I then saw England plain.
—from *The White Cliffs* by Alice Duer Miller

The RAF was always rich in slang. Some of its idiom was both technical and necessary: 'angels' always signified height, so that 'bandits seventy-plus at angels one-five' signified 'more than seventy German raiders approaching at 15,000 feet'. To 'scramble' was to take-off', to 'pancake' was to land. But many other phrases marked the idiosyncrasies of a highly individualistic emergent service. And no pilot ever crashed a plane, he 'pranged' it. If events went awry, they had 'gone for a Burton', in which case the pilot was never put out or fed up, he was 'browned off' or 'cheesed off', and this mental malaise likewise prevailed if he was called upon to 'stooge' (fly uneventfully). If his performance was erratic, too slow, or ill-conceived, he was admonished to 'take your finger out'.

In the last resort, no man among them ever died in action; he 'bought it'.

Thus, for all Dowding's pilots, September 3, 1939, was always 'the day the balloon went up', as indeed they did: 400 barrage balloons over London alone and at least fifty over coastal ports like Dover, grey, motionless. Sixty-five feet wide by twenty-five deep, linked by a perilous mesh of steel cable. There they would remain moored for the nine long months of the Phoney War or Sitzkrieg, while the pilots endured twenty-five degrees of frost in one of the coldest winters of that century.

"We used to say 'if pigs could fly' / And now they do. / I saw one sailing in the sky Some thousand feet above his sty, / A fat one too! / I scarcely could believe my eyes, So just imagine my surprise / To see so corpulent a pig / Inconsequently dance a jig Upon a cloud. / And, when elated by the show I clapped my hands and called 'Bravo!' / He turned and bowed. / Then, all at once, he seemed to flop / And dived behind a chimney-top / Out of my sight. / 'He's down', thought I; butnot at all, 'Twas only pride that had the fall: / To my delight / He rose quite gay and debonair, Resolved to go on dancing there / Both day and night. / So pigs can fly, / They really do, / This chap, though anchored in the slime, / Could reach an altitude sublime—A pig, 'tis true! / I wish I knew / Just how not only pigs but men / Might rise to nobler heights again /Right in the blue / And start anew!"—*To A Barrage Balloon* by May Morton

On September 2, squadron after squadron recorded in its diary 'We are ready for anything,' yet uneventful week succeeded uneventful week.

Despite this aerial stalemate, Air Chief Marshal Sir Hugh Dowding faced a critical dilemma. By late September, when Lord Gort's British Expeditionary Force moved across the English Channel to France, four Hurricane squadrons—Nos. 1, 73, 85, and 87—moved with them. By mid-November,

WAAFs at the launch of a barrage balloon near Garrison church, Portsmouth in 1940.

far left: If pigs could fly; left: A balloon barrage near Buckingham Palace, London, in 1940; below left: A Hawker Hurricane Mk I in 1940; right: Air Vice Marshal Sir Hugh Dowding, head of RAF Fighter Command; far right: Squadron Leader James 'Ginger' Lacey, achieved nineteen confirmed enemy aircraft shot down during the Battle of Britain and a final tally of twenty-eight confirmed kills in the Second World War.

when a German invasion of the Low Countries was rumoured, two more squadrons, the Gladiators of Nos. 607 and 615, were sent as back-up. Against a planned minimum of forty-six squadrons, Dowding was left with no more than thirty-five for home defence.

For the pilots, these, as yet were high-level concerns. In this long spell of enforced idleness, their preoccupations were as varied as the men themselves. Acting Pilot Officer Richard Hillary, soon to join No. 603 (City of Edinburgh) Squadron, arguably the most famous of all RAF 'guinea pigs', was reflecting that the fighter plane pointed "to war as it ought to be, war which is individual combat between two people … I shan't get maimed: either I shall get killed or I shall get a few pleasant putty medals and enjoy being stared at in a night club."

At Hedon Aero Club, outside Hull, Sergeant James 'Ginger' Lacey had no such consoling convictions. Within weeks, he was slated to join No. 501 (County of Gloucester) Squadron at Filton, near Bristol, yet, as he recorded in his diary, "The prospect of fighting in a war scared me stiff." The irony was palpable. In the battle to come, Lacey was to destroy more German aircraft—eighteen, including the Heinkel that bombed Buckingham Palace on September 13, 1940—than any other pilot.

Many still lamented the vanished grace-notes of peacetime. For Flying Officer Al Deere, a phlegmatic New Zealander, life with No. 54 Squadron at Hornchurch now added up to long hours at readiness, camping out in tents, humping sandbags to build dispersal pens and blast protection bays alongside civilians paid an hourly rate for the same job. At North Weald, twenty-year-old Pilot Officer Barry Sutton, of No. 56 Squadron, thought wistfully of the daily working parades, the leisurely leaves, the guest nights and the civilian clothes that had gone. Now, as a combatant-to-be, Sutton promptly sought out the Adjutant to make his will: £30 worth of belongings to his fiancée, Sylvia, his leaky two-seater Austin Seven to his cousin John.

Here's to you, as good as you are, / And here's to me, as bad as I am; / But as good as you are, and as bad as I am, / I am as good as you are, as bad as I am. —Anon. Old Scottish toast

left: Flight Lieutenant Peter Townsend with his rigger and fitter in the Battle of Britain; below: The crew of the Heinkel He 111 bomber downed by Townsend, F/O Tiger Folkes, and Sgt. James Hallowes, on 3 February 1940. It was the first enemy aircraft brought down on British soil in the Second World War.

As 1939 yielded to 1940, Dowding's was still a strangely disparate Command, a bewildering mix of confident professionals and wet-behind-the-ears novices. Pilot Officer 'Johnnie' Johnson, with No. 616 (South Yorkshire) Squadron at Coltishall, Norfolk, would ultimately enter the battle with no more than twenty-three flying hours on Spitfires in his log book. It was the same for Flying Officer David Crook, later a notable flight commander with No. 609 (West Riding) Squadron. Until December, 1939, Crook and his fellow cadets passed each evening in the bar of the New Inn, Gloucester, sweltering in their greatcoats. Their wingless tunics would have betrayed their fledgling status to the world.

At all levels, the thirst for action fought with soul-searching doubts. At Acklington, on the northeast coast, the night of January 30, 1940, saw three Flight Lieutenants of No. 43 Squadron, Peter Townsend, Caesar Hull, a chunky South African, and John Simpson launch into a wild, near-hysterical jig, La Cachita, a cross between a rumba and an apache dance, which sent chairs and tables flying. Their manic elation was understandable: each man had that day shot down the first three Heinkel bombers to crash on English soil. They had killed and they had lived to tell the tale.

"I did two patrols today and on the first I got lost and almost toured France trying to find the aerodrome, but having landed at a French aerodrome I eventually got back. We didn't see anything on either patrol but we thought we had on the latter and I got so excited. I now have had six hours sleep in forty-eight hours and haven't washed for over thirty-six hours. My God, am I tired . . . and I am up again at 3 a.m. tomorrow."
—from the diary of Pilot Officer Denis Wissler, No. 17 Squadron

A privileged few—all of them triumphant survivors of the battle to come—had early on fallen heavily for Reginald Mitchell's Spitfire Mark I. For the South African Flight Lieutenant Adolph 'Sailor' Malan, of 74 Squadron, Hornchurch, exchanging their Hawker Furies for the Spitfire at the time of Munich was "like changing over from Noah's Ark to the Queen Mary." Two months later, at Duxford, 65 Squadron's Pilot Officer Roland Robert Stanford Tuck, a slim dandy given to monogrammed silk handkerchiefs, was equally entranced. For Tuck, the Spitfire was "thirty feet of wicked beauty . . . with practically no relation to any of the aircraft I'd flown previously." So eager was he to master this answer to a fighter pilot's prayer that he patented a private mnemonic—BTFCPUR (brakes, trim, flaps, contacts, petrol, undercarriage, radiator)—which enabled him to start up a Spitfire blindfolded.

Another convert was the legendary Flying Officer Douglas Bader, who eight years earlier, after stunting in a Bulldog over Woodley Airfield, near Reading, had had both legs amputated below the knee. Incredibly, in October 1939, the twenty-nine-year-old Bader became the first man with artificial legs ever to pass a medical for General Duties, as flying was known. Posted to No. 19 Squadron, at Duxford, in February, 1940, Bader too, was soon enthralled by the way the Spitfire handled, "like a highly-strung thoroughbred."

Significantly, long before battle was joined, all three men, so at ease in their Spitfires, were more and more coming to question the Fighter Command Number 1 Attack, where fighters swung into line behind their leader, queuing to deliver a three-second attack before swinging away, their underbellies a sure target for a German rear gunner. For Malan, it was "pretty to watch and excellent for drill purposes" but totally unsuited to a Spitfire's maximum speed of 355 mph. Tuck saw what he called the tight 'guardsman' formations as counter-productive; pilots were too busy watching each other's wing-tips to keep their eyes peeled for enemy aircraft.

Bader, the most explosively outspoken of the three, presciently saw the battles to come as they would eventuate, a whirling pattern of individual dogfights with every man for himself. "The chap who'll control the battle will still be the chap who's got the height and sun, same as the last war," he dogmatized, "That old slogan of Ball, Bishop and McCudden (three Royal Flying Corps veterans, all of whom were awarded the Victoria Cross: Albert Ball, William Avery Bishop, and James Byford McCudden): 'Beware of the Hun in the sun' wasn't just a funny rhyme. Those boys learned from experience."

These tactics would ultimately be proven right, although for months to come many squadrons would continue to fly in the strange, tight formation that the Luftwaffe called "the bunch of bananas." Yet, what all three men failed to ask themselves was one salient question: would the planes in which to pursue these tactics be forthcoming from the assembly lines? In the four months from January to April 1940, the Air Ministry was to produce 2,729 aircraft—but only 638 of them were the desperately needed fighters.

On May 10, 1940, Fighter Command's salvation was at hand. At 5 a.m. on that day, the sirens screamed from Lyon to Newcastle upon Tyne; the code word René, René, René passed from army post to army post along the Belgian frontier. Hitler had struck in the west against Belgium, France, Holland, and tiny Luxembourg simultaneously. Two days earlier, a damning House of Commons debate on Britain's failure to wrest Norway—which Hitler had attacked on April 9—from Germany's grasp had toppled the Chamberlain Government. On May 10, Winston Churchill, that longtime prophet of aerial doom, became the new Premier.

It was now, to put an end to what he called "the muddle and scandal of the (Air Ministry's) aircraft production branch," that Churchill appointed the sixty-one-year-old Canadian newspaper tycoon, bustling, ruthless little William Maxwell Aitken, first Baron Beaverbrook, to the newly-created position, Minister of Aircraft Production.

From the first, "The Beaver" seemed to vie with Churchill as to how many toes he could trample on; to him, the entire Air Staff were, to the bitter end, "the bloody Air Marshals." If Beaverbrook sought storage space he snatched it from the Air Ministry without prior consultation, then padlocked it. To make aircraft factory workers feel "important" he flashed messages onto cinema screens recalling them to duty. To instil the same sense of belonging into the nation's housewives, he launched a personal campaign of "Saucepans Into Spitfires," beseeching them: "Send me your pots and pans, send me your aluminium." Whether a single Spitfire was created from the resultant cornucopia remains dubious, but in those anxious days the housewives knew a true sense of purpose.

Working from Stornaway House, St James's Park, his London home, rather than from the M.A.P. building on Millbank, Beaverbrook soon refused to adhere to any appointments schedule; all took potluck, first come, first served. Papers were piled on spare beds, typewriters were glimpsed in bathrooms, and meals, at irregular intervals during a sixteen-hour day, were delivered on trays. Often, in an office plastered with slogans—"Organisation is the Enemy of Improvisation"—"It is a Long Way from Knowing to Doing"—six officials were lined up before Beaverbrook's desk at one time with memos to present.

When he decided to merge the industrial complex of Lord Nuffield, the "British Ford," with the old-guard firm of Vickers-Armstrong, Beaverbrook despatched a secretary to haul Nuffield out of bed at midnight and break the news. Nuffield's subsequent impassioned plea to Churchill fell on deaf ears.

at top: Douglas Bader of 242 Squadron; left: Al Deere in 1990; above: Bader with Ginger Lacey, 1968.

"I cannot interfere with the manufacture of aircraft," was Churchill's firm rejoinder.

Beaverbrook's credo was aptly expressed in a letter to Sir Samuel Hoare, soon en route as ambassador-extraordinary to Franco's Spain: "I don't care if the middle classes lie sleepless in their beds, so long as the workers stay active at their benches." For what Beaverbrook sought to do, fearing the massed might of Luftwaffe bombers, was to disrupt bomber production deliberately for the sake of stockpiling fighters.

"I saw my reserves slipping away like sand in an hourglass," Dowding was to report later." ... without his (Beaverbrook's) drive behind me I could not have carried on in the battle." And Beaverbrook's figures spoke for themselves. The 638-fighter output of the Phoney War was eclipsed almost overnight. From May to August, the height of "The Beaver's" war effort, M.A.P., produced 1,875 fighters, and, thanks to the truculent persistence of one chief, Trevor Westbrook, repaired 1,872. A past master of cannibalisation, Westbrook saw to it that three damaged aircraft could ensure one fit for service; if instruments were lacking, Westbrook's solution was to unabashedly pillage RAF depots.

It was not a programme achieved without the 'blood, toil, tears and sweat' which were all that Churchill had offered the British. Robert Bruce Lockhart, who looked in on one midnight meeting of Beaverbrook and his department chiefs at Stornaway House, never forgot it. The exchanges were as staccato as machine-gun fire.

"How many planes are you producing this week? Double it!"

Any protest produced a fearsome, "Why not?"

"Because I am short of mechanics."

"How many do you need?"

"Thirty or forty."

"Which figure do you mean?"

"Thirty."

"You'll have them on Monday. Double your figure."

The urgency was appropriate. Across the Channel, within two weeks of Hitler's headlong blitzkrieg, a vast military disaster was in the making.

top left: 27-victory ace Group Captain 'Sailor' Malan; top right: Pilot Officer Al Deere (right); far left: R.J. Mitchell (centre, sitting), designer of the Spitfire, with Vickers test pilot Mutt Summers (far left) and Spitfire test pilot Jeffrey Quill (far right). left: A Mk I Spitfire during the Battle of Britain.

The Few

below: RAF Hurricane pilots ready to go; bottom left: Pilot Officer Bob Doe; bottom right: A Sergeant pilot.

Many a battle have I won in France, / When as the enemy hath been ten to one:
Why should I not now have the like success?
—from *Henry VI*, part 3, by William Shakespeare

On the late afternoon of Wednesday, May 15, Sir Hugh Dowding was a man with a mission. At this hour, the War Cabinet was once again in full session, some thirty men flanking the green baize table on the first floor of No. 10, Downing Street—among them, Dowding noted gratefully, such committed allies as Lord Beaverbrook, "the little nut-brown man," and the ruddy-faced mild-eyed Air Chief Marshal Sir Cyril Newall, Chief of the Air Staff.

Presiding over this meeting, Winston Churchill was scowling balefully—for Dowding's presence, at his own urgent request, was until now unprecedented.

At issue were the ten fighter squadrons which Churchill, on an impulse, had that very morning promised France's Premier Paul Reynaud, since the entire French front was crumbling under the onslaught of German armour. It was now, for five or ten minutes, "as elegantly as possible," that Dowding would put his case for the squadrons' retention in England—finally flinging down his pencil so forcefully that Beaverbrook was convinced he was about to resign. Then, rising from his seat, Dowding advanced deliberately on Churchill, a hastily-sketched graph in red ink clutched in his hand.

"This red line shows the wastage of Hurricanes in the last ten days," he told the Premier flatly, "If the line goes on at the same rate for the next ten days there won't be a single Hurricane left, either in France or in England."

For Dowding it seemed then that his cogent argument had won the day—as indeed, for a little under twenty-four hours, it had.

All unknown to Fighter Command's chief, Churchill, by now in Paris and again under heavy pressure from Reynaud, had agreed afresh to a reinforcement of ten squadrons—until at 11 p.m., on May 16, Sir Cyril Newall had staunchly vetoed it. Although squadrons from south-east England might rotate to French airfields in daylight hours, Newall conceded, "I do not believe that ... a few more fighter squadrons ... would make the difference between victory and defeat in France."

It was a crucial decision for the battle to come. Already in ten days fighting, 195 Hurricanes had been irretrievably lost.

For the ten Hurricane squadrons already based on French soil, their role from the first had been one of total and uncoordinated confusion. Each eighteen-hour day had seen every battle fought as an eleventh-hour emergency, attacks against bridges and light ack-ack, destined to do little more than boost the morale of the B.E.F.; at Merville, near Arras, the brief sojourn of No. 79 Squadron, despatched on May 10, was climaxed by a sunlit flarepath of tool kits, petrol tins and blazing Hurricanes. By May 24 the remnants of the squadron were back at Biggin Hill.

At first no man had cavilled at the rigours of life in the field: the sleeping in barns, the shaving in streams, that became the universal lot, where 'dispersal' now scaled down to no more than a field telephone and a ditch. Yet the sense of helplessness was everywhere apparent. On May 17, Sergeant James 'Ginger' Lacey was one of sixteen 501 Squadron pilots attacking German armour for the first time with their .303 machine-guns.

"It was like shooting at elephants with a pea-shooter," Lacey complained later. "The tank commanders didn't even pay us the compliment of closing their turrets; they just ducked their heads as we came over and stuck them out again as we'd gone past." The tank, Lacey noted, rolled on completely unscathed.

Central to the thinking that would lead to the heaviest defeat ever inflicted on a French army in the field was the defensive concept of the 400-mile-long Maginot Line, "like row upon row of sunken earthbound battleships," a line which left France both north and south naked to her enemies. It was to the south, where the heights of the Ardennes Forest had been reckoned "equal to the best fortifications," that the German armour had struck as early as the night of May 11, and this was of a piece with the seizure of Belgium's "impregnable" Fort Eben Emael by nine gliders soon after dawn on May 10, the devastation of the ancient fort of Sedan three days later. Early on May 15, as the Wehrmacht surged through the forty-mile gap south and west of Sedan, sweeping for the Channel and cutting the Allies in half, Reynaud, calling from Paris, had appealed hysterically to Churchill, "We are beaten . . . we have lost the battle."

On May 19, four days after assuming office, the new Commander-in-Chief, General Maxime Weygand, summed up for history: "This war is sheer madness. We have gone to war with a nineteen-eighteen army against a German army of nineteen-thirty-nine."

It was in essence, an epitaph for all those Hurricane squadrons that had flown from the first part of the battle. The ill-fated "B" Flight of No. 56 Squadron, detached from North Weald, was written off within seven days; one who came back, Flight Sergeant "Taffy" Higginson, reported, "It was sheer hell and terror from start to finish." At Lille-Seclin, where seventeen pilots were lost and only three pilots remained to No. 85 Squadron, one man, Sergeant 'Sammy' Allard, survived only through sheer fatigue, falling asleep three times over German-held territory, then collapsing afresh in the cockpit on landing. Finally, evacuated to England, he slept for a total of thirty hours.

All over France, in these disquieting days, the casualties, in terms of both men and machines, were mounting daily. At Le Mans, No. 501 Squadron were down to three planes; all but two were lost to No. 111 Squadron. The first into action at Vassincourt, and among the last to leave, No. 1 Squadron, returned to England in a state of mind that was near pathological. "We were convinced that the Air Ministry were holding back the £60 due for kit replacement until we'd all got killed," Pilot Officer Peter Boot recalled wonderingly, "There was a real persecution complex throughout the squadron." Some squadrons, like No. 607, where twenty-six pilots were lost, had only their inheritors to speak for them. "Things were in an awful mess," remembers Squadron Leader James Vick, who took command of 607 at Tangmere, "It was quite a shock to walk in and find that practically all of them were dead and to take over their huts and their old cars."

Few units pulled out under conditions more traumatic than No. 242, the all-Canadian fighter squadron. From early on, Flying Officer Russ Wiens had noted, "The war in the air today makes shows like Dawn Patrol look like Sunday School;" long slow weeks of attrition were to follow. Between May and June, every pilot of Flying Officer rank, all middle echelon officers, was lost over enemy territory. At Biggin Hill, the ultimate line of retreat, Pilot Officer Don Howitt spent almost all of his time re-addressing both the letters and the luggage of those who had gone missing. Not until June 14 did No. 242's rear guard, victualled only by two sacks of carrots, pull out for the coast at St Nazaire, and anxious moments followed even there. At Nantes, while their ground crews embarked, the pilots weighed in to refuel, re-arm and service their own aircraft.

Even the visiting firemen—those southcoast squadrons which in daylight hours patrolled the Arras-

top left: Hurricane control column recovered from a crash site near Chidham, England; above: A Hurricane in its revetment; left: RAF fighter pilots in 1940.

right: The Mk IX Spitfire of the Old
Flying Machine Company, Duxford,
flown by Mark Hanna.

Cambrai-Lille-St Omer sector—sensed danger in the air. "Land at Abbeville, refuel, hear dreadful stories, get very frightened," noted the diarist of Squadron Leader John Worrall's No. 32 Squadron, "do a patrol, see nothing, feel better, return to Biggin Hill, feel grand." Theirs was a charmed life. "Have just heard . . . that 605 Squadron were sent from here to cover the evacuation from Dunkirk," one flight commander wrote from Tangmere, " . . . The news has just come through that they have lost nearly all their chaps on the first day including their C.O., George Perry."

That was on May 31, and six days earlier the Secretary of State for War, Anthony Eden, had authorized Lord Gort's British Expeditionary Force to deny the French High Command who were essentially their masters and effect a wholesale withdrawal to the coast, fighting back down a corridor fifty miles long by fifteen wide to the 1,000-year-old port of Dunkirk. To heighten the crisis, on May 27, King Leopold of the Belgians, with three-quarters of his territory lost, had sought an armistice from midnight—leaving the whole left flank of the British Army open for some twenty miles. A mighty military evacuation was in the offing.

For Fighter Command this was a new and near insurmountable challenge. Ostensibly, squadrons like the Hornchurch-based No. 92 boasted a full complement of twenty-six pilots; the daily reality was a scant fourteen, young men still formally clad in the white flying overalls of peacetime, airborne in Spitfires as yet innocent of armoured plating. On any one patrol, the odds were weighted; between Calais and Dunkirk, on May 24 No. 54 Squadron, another Hornchurch unit, somehow survived an encounter with seventy German bombers and countless Messerschmitts.

It was thus no time for lone wolves. The lucky ones, like Pilot Officer Tony Woods-Scawen, limped back to Tangmere with his Hurricane's hydraulics shot to splinters, his cockpit bathed in oil, lacking even the pressure to put down his undercarriage, yet marvellously, indisputably alive. "How did you get on, sir?," his ground crew pressed him, "What was it like?," and Woods-Scawen had just one seraphic answer, "Dee-licious!"

"The conventional way to start a Hurricane was to pour a flood of electricity into the engine from a trolley-load of accumulator batteries until its twelve cylinders began to fire. Alternatively it was possible to insert a starting handle in each side and, by winding furiously, coax the engine into life. This was blistering toil. The flies danced delightedly around the pilots' sweating heads. As each fighter poppled and crackled and finally roared, it was necessary for the pilot to nurse it until it would idle happily, then lock the brakes on, jump out, and go and help someone else. Quickly, before the first plane began to overheat. There was one great incentive in getting the propellers turning. They blew away those bastard, bloodsucking French flies.
—from *Piece of Cake* by Derek Robinson

Within days, Fighter Command's Dunkirk dilemma was plain: should they stage small patrols at frequent intervals, boosting the morale of the retreating troops, or larger sporadic patrols, in the hope of coming to grips with the German bombers? Of a Spitfire's two hours and twenty minutes flying time, only twenty minutes operational manoeuvres were feasible at full throttle; on one day alone, May 30, the Hornchurch wing flew sixty-eight sorties over Dunkirk, yet never once sighted an enemy plane. It was small wonder that the station commander, Cecil Bouchier, stated: "The coverage of the beaches of Dunkirk was infinitely more exhausting and exacting than any part of the Battle of Britain."

all: The beaches of Dunkirk, France, scene of the evacuation of the British Expeditionary Force, between 27 May and 4 June 1940.

below: New Zealand's top fighter aces of the war, Colin Gray with twenty-seven kills, and Al Deere (right) with twenty-two; below right: A lobby card promoting the film *First of the Few*, about the development of the Spitfire. It featured Leslie Howard in the role of Supermarine designer R. J. Mitchell.

left: Reaching an ultimate rank of Generalleutnant, Adolf Galland rose to command the German fighter force. In 705 combat missions he shot down 104 enemy aircraft and went on to form JG44, an early jet fighter unit which flew the Messerschmitt Me 262 in limited action during the Defence of the Reich; below: Roland Robert Stanford Tuck was one of the highest achievers in the RAF during the Second World War, with twenty-nine German planes to his credit by 28 January 1942, when he was shot down and became a prisoner of war. His postwar friendship with Galland led to the German becoming godfather to Tuck's son in 1966.

After ten days of intensive operations, some squadrons had to be withdrawn from the line. The seven remaining planes of No. 54 Squadron under Flight Lieutenenat James Leathart flew north for a well-earned rest to Catterick, Yorkshire, where a puzzled senior officer greeted them, "Which flight is this?" Replying, Leathart spoke at that moment for the whole hard-pressed RAF, "Flight, nothing. This is a squadron."

How a pilot viewed the shameful glory of Dunkirk depended, invariably, on temperament. For Flight Lieutenant John Simpson, a happy-go-lucky extravert, what stood out was the holiday aspect: "I could see the *Brighton Belle*, and the paddle steamers, and the sort of cheerful little boats you see calling at coastal towns on Sunday. Hundreds of boats! Fishing boats and motor boats, and Thames river craft and strings of dinghies, being towed by bigger boats. All packed with troops, and people standing in the water ..." But Flying Officer Robert Stanford Tuck, a by-then case-hardened realist of No. 92 Squadron, glimpsed a harsher picture, from 1,000 feet above the harbour—" ... shells exploding on the cluttered beach, raising tall white plumes in the shallow water ... smouldering trucks and carriers, ruptured convoys, abandoned stores piled ready for burning ... sandbags being filled for the last dour stand ..."

Probably no man in the fleeting moments of patrol, could grasp the cold hard logistics of this victory-in-defeat: from a triangle less than 1,000 miles square, some 366,000 men would be ferried to safety by more than 1,000 vessels, ranging from sleek whippet-like destroyers to cockle boats from the Essex mud flats. Travelling in garbage trucks and on children's scooters, on tractors and astride dairy cattle, the remnants of an army were drawn by one landmark: the column of black smoke, visible from thirty miles away, that marked the beaches of Dunkirk.

These were military concerns. For the pilots, the lowering skies above twenty-three miles of sandy shelving shore now became a proving ground for RAF and Luftwaffe alike—nor was this a challenge that the Luftwaffe, despite the battle scars of Spain and Poland viewed lightly. The veterans among them saw to that. At Wissant, near Calais, Oberst Theo Osterkamp, regional fighter commander for Air Fleet Two, gave due warning to one flight leader, Hauptmann Walter Kienzle, "Now we are going to fight 'The Lords,' and that is something else again. They are hard fighters and they're good fighters— even though our machines are better."

Some Germans learned this lesson by degrees. For Hauptmann Werner Mölders, leader of Fighter Group 53's First Wing, with fourteen confirmed "kills" from the Spanish Civil War, the first stages of the Battle of France had been almost tiresomely routine. No sooner did the hapless Hurricanes abandon an airfield than Mölders' acolytes, Leutnant Claus and Oberleutnant Kaluza, armed only with tommy guns, landed in their Fieseler-Storch and took over. "Keep a stiff upper lip, boys, even if you have to wedge it down with a matchstick," Mölders would rally them, though still knowing that morale was at its peak.

It was the bomber pilots who first gave the RAF their due. "They were the real resistance, those fighters," acknowledged Oberleutnant Karl Kessel, of the Second Bomber Group's First Wing. "They came from above, and from below, from the sides and from everywhere—and this was something we were meeting for the first time." Leutnant Otto Wolfgang Bechtle, of the Group's Third Wing, concurred: "We knew about the Spitfires and respected them even before the war. We respected them even more after Dunkirk."

Ironically, for many German pilots, it was suddenly a cleaner battle once the RAF entered the fray.

Ground strafing the beaches from 300 feet Hauptmann Paul Temme of the Second Fighter Group's First Wing felt nothing but revulsion—"just unadulterated killing ... cold-blooded point-blank murder." Hans Heinz Brustellin, of the 51st Group, felt the same. "It was an awful business if you looked too closely, a demoralizing business for a fighter force. Some got physically sick with the killing."

No Luftwaffe ace felt this more keenly than Hauptmann Adolf Galland, a Spanish Civil War ace credited with seventeen victories, then part of the 27th Fighter Wing. "My first kill was child's play," Galland recalled of a one-sided combat with a Belgian piloting a beat-up Hurricane. "I had something approaching a twinge of conscience." His first brush with the RAF revealed a new kind of adversary—"Each relentless aerial combat was a question of 'you' or 'me'. Until then we'd always been army support planes. Dunkirk gave us our first chance to prove ourselves. Dunkirk should have been an emphatic warning for the leaders of the Luftwaffe." One such alarm bell was sounded on May 29, when Galland, escorting the wing's commander, crusty old Oberstleutnant Max Ibel, was jumped by a gaggle of Spitfires. Although he came instantly to Ibel's aid, "blazing away with all I had," the Spitfires totally ignored this brash intruder. "Sure of their target, they streaked single mindedly after Ibel, who was lucky to survive a crash landing."

I'm a lean dog, a keen dog, a wild dog and lone: / I'm a rough dog, a tough dog, hunting on my own: I'm a bad dog, a mad dog, teasing silly sheep: / I love to sit and bay the moon, to keep fat souls from sleep.
—*Lone Dog* by Irene R. MacLeod

Tributes like Galland's would then have astonished the RAF. Trained to fly pre-war copybook attacks in rigid air display formation, the fluid, weaving tactics of the Messerschmitts had them dazed. Flying Officer John Petre of No. 19 Squadron, a star pupil of the RAF College at Cranwell, was on the tail of an ME 109 when he recoiled abruptly; an explosive bullet had torn into his cockpit, shattering his instrument panel.

Plunging into a spin dive below the level of the swarm, Petre realized that he had never even seen the plane that hit him.

At this stage of the battle, as the RAF saw it, sheer audacity rather than tactics saw them through. Squadron Leader Teddy Donaldson, of No. 151 Squadron, was closing on a Heinkel over Dunkirk when he found his ammo exhausted; still, in cold fury, he rammed his Hurricane forward. His nerve gone, the German pilot first jettisoned his bombs, then bailed out minus his parachute.

On another such sortie, Robert Stanford Tuck, soon to command No. 92 Squadron, was exasperated beyond belief; the din of voices in his earphones testified not only to lack of radio discipline, but to the total confusion then prevailing.

"Look out—here's another!"

"Watch that bastard—smack underneath you, man, under you!"

"He's burning—I got him, I got him, chaps."

"Bloody hell, I've been hit ..."

"Jesus, where are they all coming from?"

"For God's sake, somebody ..."

This archetypal cry for help symbolized the bewilderment of all the novices; a gut reaction against

top'' RAF calisthenics in 1940; left:
Fighter pilots as subjects in a recruiting
poster in 1941; above: The pilot's view
through the gunsight of a Spitfire.

judgements more fleeting than they had ever been called upon to make, in combats so dizzying as to defy gravity. "The ME 109s were quicksilver," pointed out Squadron Leader 'Tubby' Mermagen, a portly teddy bear of a man, leading No. 222 Squadron out of Hornchurch, "It would have been ideal to come against them as a controlled formation, but the Germans always split up, so somehow you did, too." To this, Mermagen added the bleak corollary, "It was every man for himself then—which was all right if you were good."

Barely a handful would have rated that accolade as Dunkirk dawned. Yet just as the Luftwaffe learned wariness and grudging respect following their first encounters, Dowding's pilots too, grew more cunning. Over Dunkirk, just as later over London, the sure tactic was to ignore the gleaming arrowhead of Messerschmitts 4,000 feet above them. The secret was to carve into the bomber formations before they could ever reach their target. Among the first to score, as Tuck would always remember, was his own squadron, No. 92. At 12,000 feet, inland from Dunkirk, they spied twenty Dornier 17s curving gently to starboard, lining up for their bombing run against the huddled troops. It was then that Flying Officer Anthony Bartley did, as Tuck put it, " a rather extraordinary thing. He went down the starboard side of the stream, shooting them up one wing, and I distinctly saw him leapfrog over one 'vic', under the next, then up over the third—and so on. He did the whole side of the formation like that, and he tumbled at least one—maybe two—as flamers at that single pass. It was just about the cheekiest bit of flying I'd seen. The chaps in his section tried to follow him, but they managed only one or two of the jumps. Tony made every one."

Most survivors later gave thanks to Dunkirk as a salutary baptism of fire. For on Saturday June 1st, the last full-scale day of the evacuation, they were almost 3,000 sorties wiser, and they were out for blood. As early as five a.m. 4,000 feet above the target, the dawn patrol of three Spitfire squadrons saw the strength of the opposition: no bombers were in sight but the grey shapes of a dozen Me 109s and ME 110s were darting like sharks from cloud cover. By now even the fighters held no terror for them; within seconds battle was joined.

By six a.m., claiming a total bag of fifteen German fighters, the dawn patrol was heading back for base.

Then, just as suddenly as it had begun, it was all over. On June 4, thirteen days before eighty-four-year-old Marshal Henri Phillipe Pétain, France's new premier, sought an armistice, a single flight of No. 242 Squadron was airborne over Dunkirk. More than 50,000 vehicles littered the beaches and the promenades, choking the inshore waters and smoke still billowed from the burning port, but not a soul moved in the streets. Only the white sail of a lone yacht, moving towards the open sea, caught their attention.

There was nothing to indicate that the nine days of Dunkirk had cost Dowding 106 fighters and that only 283 planes then remained serviceable for the nation's defence.

Already the promises had been made, no less than the prophesies. On June 4 Churchill had pledged the nation to "fight on the beaches . . . on the landing grounds . . . in the fields and in the streets." On June 18, he warned: "The Battle of France is over. I expect the Battle of Britain is about to begin." It was General Sir Hastings Ismay, Assistant Secretary to the War Cabinet, who put it more starkly to the U.S. Military attaché, General Raymond Lee. "The future of our Western civilization rests on the shoulders of the Royal Navy and about 5,000 pink-cheeked young pilots."

An RAF fighter pilot trying to relax between sorties at his fighter station in southern England during World War Two.

Some of The Few

War artist Captain Cuthbert Orde drew and painted many RAF airmen, including Adolph 'Sailor' Malan, the great South African air leader.

Seven-victory ace Noel Agazarian flew Spitfires with 609 Squadron at Warmwell, Dorset. His sister, Monique, flew in the Air Transport Auxiliary.

Willy Rhodes-Moorhouse downed ten enemy aircraft before being shot down and killed on 6 September 1940.

'Cocky' Dundas was a Wing Commander at age twenty-two, and one of the most respected officers in the Royal Air Force.

Known as 'Cats Eyes', John Cunningham was possibly the greatest British nightfighter pilot of the war. He was given command of 604 Squadron and later, of 85 Squadron.

A great Polish fighter ace of the Battle of Britain, Witold Urbanowicz was credited with seventeen enemy aircraft in the Second World War.

Some of The Few

Douglas Bader, who lost his legs in a pre-war flying accident, famously led 242 (Canadian) Squadron in the Battle of Britain.

Thirteen kills were credited to Bobby Oxspring in the war. He commanded 91 and 222 Squadrons, as well as RAF Gatow, Berlin, after the war.

John Peel commanded No. 145 Squadron at Tangmere in the Battle of Britain period. He commanded the Kenley Wing in 1941.

Brendan 'Paddy' Finucane, a twenty-eight victory ace, drowned when he had to ditch in the English Channel after being hit by ground fire on 15 July 1942.

A twenty-eight victory ace was James 'Ginger' Lacey, the second highest-scoring RAF Battle of Britain pilot. Lacey downed a German bomber that had attacked Buckingham Palace.

Frederick 'Taffy' Higginson had tallied fifteen aerial victories by the time he was shot down over Lille in 1941.

Some of The Few

A.V. Clowes painted a wasp on his Hurricane and added a stripe to it with each enemy aircraft he brought down in the war.

Victor Beamish took command at RAF North Weald in June 1940 and flew operationally with his squadrons whenever he could.

'Sammy' Allard shot down nineteen German aircraft in his distinguished wartime career.

Ronald Kellett commanded 303 (Polish) Squadron in the Battle of Britain.

John C. Mungo-Park flew with 'Sailor' Malan's 74 Squadron at Hornchurch. He was shot down and killed on 27 June 1941 north of Dunkirk. He was credited with eleven aerial victories.

Stan Turner achieved fourteen aerial victories in his service with 242, 145, 411, and 249 Squadrons in the second World War.

Some of The Few

Whitney Straight served with 601 Squadron in the Battle of Britain and went on to command 242 Squadron.

Harry Broadhurst held many RAF commands in the Second World War and after, and flew in the Battle of France and the Battle of Britain.

R.R.Stanford Tuck destroyed twenty-nine enemy aircraft in the Second World War. In the postwar years he became a friend of Adolf Galland.

Raymond Duke-Woolley received two British DFCs, one American DFC, and a British DSO in his World War Two service.

H.M. Stephen accounted for at least twenty-two aerial victories between May 1940 and October 1941.

Al Deere of New Zealand accounted for twenty-two German aircraft and was a Biggin Hill Wing Leader in World War Two.

Junkers Ju 87 Stuka dive-bombers attacking in the Battle of Britain.

Channel Convoy Attacks

Later than many, earlier than some, / I knew the die was cast—that war must come; That war must come. Night after night I lay / Steeling a broken heart to face the day / When he, my son—would tread the very same / Path that his father trod. When the day came / I was not steeled—not ready. Foolish, wild / Words issued from my lips—'My child, my child, / Why should you die for England too? / He smiled: Is she not worth it, if I must? he said. / John would have answered yes—but John was dead.
—from *The White Cliffs* by Alice Duer Miller

Early on Wednesday June 5, two high-ranking Luftwaffe staff officers were picking their way through the detritus that littered the beaches east of Dunkirk: thousands of pairs of shoes discarded by fugitive soldiers, hundreds of bicycles, heavy guns silted over with sand, a blizzard of army papers stirring in the chill dawn wind. Ahead of them loomed a glinting mountain of empty wine and whisky bottles, seemingly the remnants of a last officers' mess party. It was the cue for General Hoffman von Waldau, the junior of the two, to prod the bottles contemptuously with a highly polished boot, gesturing towards the Channel. "Here is the grave of the British hopes in this war!" he prophesied, "and these," with an arrogant dismissive glance at the bottles—"are the gravestones!"

But his superior, General Erhard Milch, a dark and fleshy World War I veteran, and the Luftwaffe's Inspector General, shook a troubled head. "They are not buried yet," he remarked. Then, almost as if to himself, he added, "We have no time to waste."

It was a point that Milch was to stress urgently later that day to his chief, Feldmarschall Hermann Goering, in his private train, a few miles from Dunkirk. Yet given the euphoria prevailing after the rout of the B.E.F., Milch was painfully conscious of being a spectre at the feast. And it was with mounting perplexity that Goering heard his deputy's recommendation: "I strongly advise the immediate transfer to the Channel coast of all available Luftwaffe forces ... the invasion of Great Britain should begin without delay ... I warn you, Herr Feldmarschall, if you give the English three or four weeks to recoup, it will be too late."

Goering's first reaction was a terse *Nicht lösbar* (It won't work), and at the topmost level, Hitler, already tendering peace feelers through such sources as the Papal Nuncio in Switzerland and King Gustav of Sweden, was equally lukewarm. Not until July 16, when the British had stubbornly rejected all his offers, did the Führer issue his famous Directive No. 16: "As England, in spite of her hopeless military situation, still shows no signs of willingness to come to terms, I have decided to prepare, and if necessary to carry out, a landing operation against her." The code-name for this "exceptionally daring undertaking"—a full-scale thirteen-division invasion on a 225-mile front from Ramsgate, on the Kentish coast, to Lyme Regis, west of the Isle of Wight—was Operation Sealion.

Inevitably, there were preliminaries. Seaways like the English Channel must be closed to shipping. Ports must be brought to a standstill. Above all, the directive stressed, "the British Air Force must be eliminated to such an extent that it will be incapable of putting up any sustained opposition to the invading troops."

The main attack plan—*Adlerangriff*, or Attack of the Eagles, to come into force on receipt of the codeword *Adler Tag* (Eagle Day)—was scattered along the whole invasion front, and by the yardstick of the Polish and French campaigns, the RAF should be out of the picture in four days flat.

If the RAF were still seen as formidable adversaries, this was an unlooked for role. Despite the get-up-and-go tactics of Lord Beaverbrook's Ministry of Aircraft Production, the 283 fighters that were Dowding's standby when Dunkirk fell stood at no more than 600 by July. The other services were in worse shape still. Against Germany's 200 divisions, Britain could now muster but a score. At least ten divisions had left their heavy guns and howitzers gutted or strewn across the fields of Flanders. Out of 200 naval destroyers only seventy-four were out of dockyard hands.

The Atlantic U-boat war was fast becoming, in Churchill's words, "the only thing that ever frightened me." June alone had seen 300,000 tons of shipping lost to the torpedoes of Konteradmiral Karl Doenitz, whose fifty-seven U-boat skippers would always remember this as *Die Glückliche Zeit*, (The Happy Time). Since January their successes had been reflected on every British breakfast table—now limited to two ounces of tea a week, four of butter, half a pound of sugar.

The contention of the isolationist U.S. Ambassador, Joseph P. Kennedy, that "to suppose the Allies have much to fight with except courage is fallacious," drew a storm of protest in Foreign Office

Reichsmarschall Hermann Goering headed the German Air Force during the Battle of Britain and, in 1941, Adolf Hitler designated Goering as his successor and deputy in all offices.

44

circles—"I thought my daffodils were yellow until I met Joe Kennedy," was one abrasive reaction. Yet Air Marshal Dowding, at Fighter Command, had been equally realistic: "The Germans could lay large areas of our big towns in ruins at any time they choose to do so."

A cartoon by David Low in the London Evening Standard summed up the mood of the nation: a steel helmeted Tommy shaking a defiant fist across a storm-tossed Channel, above the caption, "VERY WELL, ALONE!"

For the first time since the Napoleonic Wars, Britons felt consciously beleaguered and they responded to the challenge with zest. As early as May 14, Anthony Eden's radio appeal for what he privately called "a broomstick army," known as the Local Defence Volunteers, had been answered with alacrity by 500,000 men. Soon to be re-christened the "Home Guard" by Churchill—and known to a later generation as "Dad's Army"—the force consisted of any man not in uniform, aged between sixteen and sixty-five, committed to a minimum of ten hours a week standing guard duty or scouting for paratroops. Overnight, as they mustered on their first parades, the England they knew was becoming a honeycomb of ghost towns, as signposts, village signs and street names came down—an idea to fox potential invaders dreamed up by the thriller writer Dennis Wheatley in a strategic memo to the War Cabinet. In reality, it baffled few more truly than the 117,000 London school children evacuated to remote villages by the Great Western Railway.

Already pillboxes, three and a half feet of solid concrete bulked as tank traps in thousands of village streets. In thousands of back gardens, the citizens had prudently installed corrugated iron shelters, six feet long and four feet deep, topped with eighteen inches of rammed earth, named after their creator, David Anderson, as an overnight haven if Goering's bombers should come.

"We were all told to plug 'Hitler is irrevocably committed to invasion'" recalled Vera Arlett, one of a team of Ministry of Information lecturers touring the south coast but on one visit to Kent, Edward R. Murrow, the tall immaculate head of the CBS network in Europe, saw few overt signs of disaster. "Most of the talk is about this year's hop harvest, the heavy oat crops, and the need for preserving fruit and vegetables for the winter..."

As always, Murrow was reporting the mood truly: in a countryside that had abruptly harked back to the era of Thomas Hardy, the British were swift to adapt. At Cadborough Farm, Rye, Sussex, the mooted invasion area for Army Group A, the farmer, John Hacking, still escorted his wife Anne, to weekly dances, but in a horse drawn cart now that petrol was short. Two miles northwest of Hawkinge airfield, surely a priority target for the Luftwaffe, Earl Knight, the tractor driver at Ladwood Farm, worked on steadily as always with his new Fordson tractor. But now a galvanized iron canopy was rigged above his head to screen him from falling shrapnel, and he steered the tractor cautiously—intent on evading the long black poles, placed to repel anticipated glider landings, that jutted from the ripening wheat.

It was a time of exodus, even so. West of Folkstone, 100,000 sheep had been evacuated from the low-lying Romney Marshes. The children had gone too, with Mickey Mouse gas masks for the toddlers, to make it all seem a game. All along the Kentish coast, house after house stood empty, often abandoned so hastily that beds were left unmade and ham and eggs congealed on the stoves—"I never thought I'd see sights like that in my home town," marvelled Mrs Lillian Ivory, who stayed resolutely put in her own hotel, the Mecca, at Folkstone.

It was a time of waiting too. By noon on August 7, it was nine days since a destroyer, let alone a

Characteristic of the Ju 87 Stuka dive-bomber, far left, were its inverted gull wings, its spatted undercarriage, and its 'Jericho trumpet' whaling siren; top centre: Crew running to their Heinkel He 111 bomber in 1940; left: Ground personnel decorate the tail fin of a Junkers Ju 88 bomber participating in the Channel attacks on Allied shipping; below far left: Uffz. Leo Zaunbrecher (second from left) and other pilots of JG 52 in the summer of 1940; left centre: In the cockpit of a Messerschmitt Bf 109 fighter, mainstay of the German Air Force in the Battle of Britain; left: Luftwaffe loaders embellishing a bomb destined for delivery on a British target in the summer of 1940.

below: Peter Townsend during the making of the film Battle of Britain in 1968; right: Caesar Hull at Tangmere; far right: Adolf Galland is assisted on a French airfield in 1940; below: RAF pilots at their ease between sorties.

Scenes in the manufacture and assembly of bomber aircraft in Germany during the Second World War. At far left: Heinkel He 111s; left: Junkers Ju 87 Stuka dive-bombers; below: Junkers Ju 88s on their assembly line.

coastal convoy, had moved in the English Channel. At his headquarters in a stuffy omnibus at Cap Blanc Nez near Wissant, Oberst Johannes Fink, the newly appointed *Kanalkampfführer* or Channel Battle Leader, was more than content. He had fulfilled his task—to win and keep air superiority over the Straits of Dover—in exactly twenty-seven days.

In vain, fighter pilots like Adolf Galland had roamed above southeast England, using height and sun as they willed it, hoping to provoke a British reaction. But none was forthcoming. Even *lockvögel*—literally decoy birds, bombers acting as bait, had produced no results. "*Schweinerei*," said Galland, in retrospect, "but still they didn't come!"

Then quite suddenly, late on the night of August 7, they did. The British had now accepted that they must "force" the Channel passage, and accordingly, at 9 p.m., C.W.9, a twenty-five-strong convoy of merchantmen had set out from Southend, on the Thames Estuary, bound for the wharves of Portsmouth and Southampton. Their cargo formed part of the 40,000 tons of seaborne coal and coke which fuelled southern industry each week. Their escort by night was a small flotilla of *Hunt* class destroyers; by day the onus of their safety would rest on Dowding's Fighter Command.

But at 1.30 a.m. on August 8, long before daylight, a German E-boat flotilla found them—fast 103-foot motor torpedo boats resembling American Coast Guard cutters. What followed was inevitable, as Captain J.H. Potts of the collier *Betswood*, 1,350 tons, would always recall, "They ravaged it like wolves from Beachy Head to the Nab Tower."

Another master, William Henry Dawson, of the 500-ton coaster *John M.*, took up the tale: "I saw a blinding flash, followed by a heavy explosion in the starboard column of the convoy. A second later the same thing happened out in the port column. The explosions rocked the ships and I could smell the cordite fumes blown over on the wind. 'What the hell's happening now?', I thought."

At first light, Dawson knew. Convoy C.W. 9 was now a convoy in name only: nothing but tiny groups of ships, scattered beyond hope of reassembly, all the way from Dover to St Catherine's Point, the southernmost tip of the Isle of Wight. Before 9 a.m., news of their passage reached the Cherbourg headquarters of the Luftwaffe's 8th Flying Corps, and its commander, *Generalmajor* the Baron von Richtofen. A trigger-tempered disciplinarian, and the cousin of Manfred 'The Red Baron' von Richtofen, the WWI air ace. The baron invariably expected 100 per cent success from each sortie—akin to that which his Stuka dive-bombers had achieved at Dunkirk. His order was peremptory: "This convoy must be wiped out."

The Stukas needed no second bidding. As the *Betswood*'s Captain Potts remembered it later: "The scene changed in an instant, from a perfectly flat sea to a typhoon." Somehow, despite the maelstrom of churning water, the *Betswood* steamed on unscathed, her sole armament a single Lewis gun on her bridge, but few other merchantmen were so lucky. "Away to starboard another flight was diving down. Swallowing hard, I saw them come ... then this salvo crashed. The first one hit the water near the starboard bow, the other was a near-miss amidships ... down came more bombs, flinging up great columns of water nearly one hundred feet high ... I saw one water column, green between me and the sun, smash over the forecastle head and sweep two gunners off their feet ... In the middle of the party, the mate dashed into the wheelhouse, shoved the man away from the wheel, and shouted, 'For God's sake, let me do something.' "

It was now, from Hornchurch in the east to Middle Wallop in the west, that Fighter Command's six sector controllers alerted their squadrons, although one unit, Squadron Leader John Peel's No. 145

above: The pilot and navigator of a Heinkel bomber en route to England in the summer of 1940; below: An RAF Spitfire pilot races to his aircraft which has been started and is ready for him.

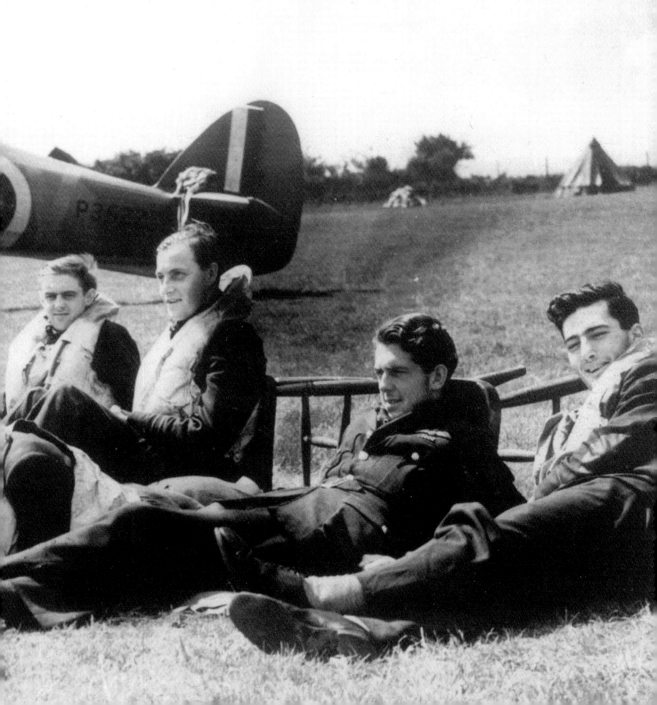

previous spread: RAF pilots between sorties in summer 1940; left: Hurricanes about to land after a patrol during the Battle of Britain; bottom left: Servicing a Hurricane at Exeter in 1940; below: The famous Rolls-Royce Merlin engine whose variants powered the Spitfire, Hurricane, Lancaster, Mosquito, and the American Mustang.

Squadron, was already in position. At 16,000 feet above St Catherine's Point they had sighted the Stukas streaking for the shipping at the moment John Peel, appropriately, gave the huntsman's cry, "Tally-ho!"

As if on cue, twelve hump-backed Hurricanes altered course, heading not for the shattered convoy but for the brassy ingot of the sun that swam above them. If they dived from the sun, Peel knew, the Germans' vision would be dazzled from the start.

Soon they were 18,000 feet above the water and again Peel's voice rasped through the intercom—'Come on chaps, down we go!" and suddenly, as the Hurricanes swooped, ninety-six .303 Browning machine-guns were chattering as one, marking the first shots, many sources maintain, to be fired in the Battle of Britain.

It was the rankest injustice, reflected Captain Dawson later, that their appearance was at once hailed by his Lewis gunner above the wheelhouse: "Here come the Spitfires!" The legend of 'invincible Spitfires' would be a long time a-dying.

From the bridge of the John M, Dawson now had a ringside view of "the grandest sight I have ever seen . . . the sky was simply full of whirling aircraft and falling, flaming black streaks of crashing dive-bombers . . . " And high above the zig-zagging convoy, the pilots of 145 Squadron were equally conscious that luck was with them. Days earlier, Flight Lieutenant Roy Dutton had broken a carpal bone in his right hand, an injury so painful he could barely press the starter button. Yet twice he found himself positioned behind slow-moving Stukas, with just enough strength to press the firing button for four long seconds, time enough to see them spin like spent bullets for the sea. This was Dutton's all-too-brief taste of battle: for six months after that his right hand was encased in plaster.

Even a novice like nineteen-year-old James Storrar, now a Cheshire veterinarian, felt himself a world-beater; opening fire on a Stuka, he barely realized that he had hit it until he saw the rear machine-gun tilting skywards and the gunner lolling dead. Convinced that they had knocked down twenty-one German planes single-handed, the squadron that night threw an all-ranks party to end them all—as Storrar recalled it, "The floor literally swam in beer." With quiet satisfaction, John Peel inscribed one swastika in his log book. The old World War One adage, "Beware of the Hun in the sun" had once again been proven true, the battle seemed almost over.

But scores of Dowding's planes, on August 8, had never seen 'the Hun in the sun'. The canny tactics of 145 Squadron had quite eluded them. Flying Officer Edward Hogg, of 151 Squadron, remembered this day; weaving his Spitfire above the foundering convoy, he had to break form combat time and again without firing a shot. However high he climbed, there were always ME 109s still higher—and all the timethe sun struck at his eyes like white fire.

To most pilots aloft, it seemed that the Luftwaffe held the sky. And even at mid-afternoon, von Richtofen's third and last sortie, an umbrella of planes filling the sky all the way to Cherbourg, struck Pilot Officer Frank Carey, of 43 Squadron, as "a raid so terrible and inexorable it was like trying to stop a steam roller." The simile was valid. Within minutes, with two pilots wounded, and two seriously injured, 43 Squadron was out of the combat.

In retrospect, the lesson was plain. Every squadron over southern England had been scrambled too late and too low. As yet, few sector controllers realized that height, above all, was what the squadrons needed—and while the Germans were timing each sortie to strike with the sun behind them, the Sector Ops Rooms did not even plot the position of the sun on their boards.

One of the world's first terror weapons, the Ju 87 Stuka dive-bomber, above, had production of more than 5,700 aircraft by its end of manufacture in 1944; left: The Messerschmitt Bf 110 two-seat day and night fighter and ground attack aircraft.

"… our machines were being warmed up. The voice of the controller came unhurried over the loud-speaker, telling us to take off, and in a few seconds we were running for our machines. I climbed into the cockpit of my plane and felt an empty sensation of suspense in the pit of my stomach. For one second time seemed to stand still and I stared blankly in front of me. I knew that that morning I was to kill for the first time. That I might be killed or in any way injured did not occur to me. Later, when we were losing pilots regularly, I did consider it in an abstract way when on the ground; but once in the air, never. I knew it could not happen to me. I suppose every pilot knows that, knows it cannot happen to him; even when he is taking off for the last time, when he will not return, he knows that he cannot be killed. I wondered idly what he was like, this man I would kill. Was he young, was he fat, would he die with the Führer's name on his lips, or would he die alone, in that last moment conscious of himself as a man? I would never know. Then I was being strapped in, my mind automatically check-ing the controls, and we were off."
—from *The Last Enemy* by Richard Hillary

Pilot Officer D.H. 'Nobby' Clarke, a Coastal Command pilot surveying the wreckage of C.W. 9 from an ROC target-towing plane above the Isle of Wight, thought in terms of a total Luftwaffe victory: "The wreckage stretched in every direction … tables, chairs, timber, hatches, spars … coke …vast rafts of it, grey-black against the dark blue of the sea … patches of oil, too, silver-grey in the sun … and ships, empty shells of red-glowing coal."

This was not an estimate shared by Hauptmann Werner Andres, an ME 109 pilot of Major Max Ibel's 27th Fighter Group, a hapless casualty of von Richtofen's last sortie. Swimming steadily in the choppy waters, thirty miles northwest of Cherbourg, Andres had never even seen the plane that had hit him—but the equation of the day's battle was to him as chilling as the icy Channel.

To be sure, 300 planes—the 8th Flying Corps, plus Ibel's fighters—had crippled or sunk twenty-two merchant ships, 70,000 tons of shipping, but all this had been achieved at a loss of thirteen Luft-waffe planes. A battle timed to last four days now loomed as a deadly war of attrition, until each side groped bloodily to a standstill.

At HQ Fighter Command, pacing his high Georgian office facing south towards the spire of Har-row Church, Air Chief Marshal Sir Hugh Dowding knew the same sense of perturbation. The losses of August 8—nineteen planes—was the highest that Fighter Command had ever been called upon to bear.

So if Goering, newly appointed Reichsmarschall, decided to step up the pressure, what could Dowding do? Exactly twenty-three squadrons existed to defend southern England, but if their losses reached a constant drain of twenty aeroplanes a day, could Beaverbrook's M.A.P. keep pace? A *Col-liers'* magazine article by the Anglophile American war correspondent, Quentin Reynolds, proclaimed, "It's still Churchill's Channel—but was it?"

For thousands, the battle had barely started, and Dowding could not know.

above: The slow but reliable Junkers Ju 52 transport workhorse of the WW2 Luftwaffe; below: A Messerschmitt Bf 109 fighter that has been brought down on the Channel coast of France in 1940.

Oberleutnant Hans Philipp was the fourth Luftwaffe fighter pilot to be credited with 100 aerial victories in the Second World War.

In more than 500 combat missions, Hauptmann Joachim Muncheberg shot down 135 enemy planes, forty-six of them Spitfires.

Werner Mölders was the leading German fighter ace in the Spanish Civil War and the first pilot in history to claim 100 victories. He was killed in the crash of a Heinkel He 111.

Another Luftwaffe bomber pilot, Joachim Helbig saw action in Poland, the Netherlands, and the Battles of France and Britain.

German nightfighter ace Egmont Prinz zur Lippe-Weissenfeld was credited with fifty-one aerial victories.

A Luftwaffe bomber pilot, Walter Storp, survived the war with the rank of Generalmajor.

Oberleutnant Erich Schuster was a veteran of the Battles of Belgium and Crete, the siege of Leningrad, and the Tunisia campaign.

Hauptmann Wilhelm Balthasar, a forty-victory ace, was killed in 1941 when a wing failed on his Bf 109 F 4 near St Omer, France.

Oberst Hajo Herrmann, a bomber pilot, flew 320 missions and sank twelve ships for a total of 70,000 tons.

Günther Rall was the third most successful fighter ace in history, with 275 kills in 621 combat missions.

Major Gordon Gollob was a Staffelkapitän in Bf 110 Zerstorers with 3/ZG 76 and 2/JG 3 during the Battle of Britain.

Oberst Hannes Trautloft flew 560 combat sorties and was credited with fifty-eight aerial victories during the Battles of France, Britain, and Operation Barbarossa.

Men of the Luftwaffe

Generalfeldmarschall Hugo Sperrle commanded Luftflotte 3 during The Battle of Britain and the Blitz.

Oberst Hermann Graf claimed 212 aerial victories in 830 combat missions and was the first fighter pilot in history to claim 200 aerial victories.

With 152 aerial victories, Hans Beisswenger was the 34th highest scoring Luftwaffe pilot of the Second World War.

Hauptmann Konrad Kahl was awarded the Knight's Cross of the Iron Cross after an operation against Allied convoy PQ17.

An unidentified pilot of Erprobungs-gruppe 210 in 1940.

Reichsmarschall and Ministerpresi-dent Hermann Goering, Luftwaffe chief, in the Battle of Britain period.

Men of the Luftwaffe

Feldwebel Horst Petzschler flew Me 109s and Fw 190s with X/JG 51.

Luftwaffe ace Adolf Galland rose to become General of the Fighter Arm of the German Air Force.

Joachim Kirschner claimed 170 aerial victories by the time he was shot down over Croatia in December 1943.

Hans Jeschonnek was Chief of the General Staff of the Luftwaffe in the time of the Battles of France and Britain.

Heinz Baer flew more than 1,000 combat missions, was shot down eighteen times and credited with at least 220 aerial victories.

Generalfeldmarschall Albert Kesselring commanded the German Air Forces in all the major German air campaigns of the war.

Some transmission towers of RAF Fighter Command's Chain Home radar system.

Hitting the Radar Chain

Hauptmann Walter Rubensdörffer was a deeply preoccupied man on the morning of Tuesday August 12. As his colleague, Oberleutnant Otto Hintze, would later recall, Rubensdörffer, a tall dynamic Swiss, aged thirty, with an infectious sense of humour, was in no mood for small talk as he sipped his breakfast coffee at Calais-Marck airfield. That morning, Rubensdorffer's twenty-eight-strong unit, Erprobungsgruppe (Test Group) 210 had been assigned to what most pilots knew could be the battle's most crucial mission.

A onetime Stuka pilot, Rubensdörffer had long nurtured the theory that fighters—whether ME 109s or ME 110s—were not only capable of carrying bombs but of hitting their targets. Faced with the profound scepticism of most Luftwaffe chiefs—foremost among them Generalfeldmarschall Albert Kesselring, Chief of Luftflotte Two Rubensdörffer had still persisted. At Rechlin, on the Baltic, he and his group of hand-picked pilots, had spent long weeks of trial and error and finally seen their perseverance pay off.

As recently as yesterday, Rubensdörffer's mixed force of 109s and 110s had swooped on a convoy code-named 'Booty', fifteen miles southeast of Harwich, to attract only sporadic ack-ack: fighter planes, the British had plainly reasoned, could do little harm to shipping. Yet Test Group 210 had scored mortal hits on two large freighters with 250-kilo bombs, then once again, engaged by 'Sailor' Malan's 74 Squadron from Hornchurch, resumed their role as fighters. The element of surprise had been all; two of Malan's pilots did not return.

Ironically, Test Group 210 was now Kesselring's most cherished unit; the man nicknamed 'Smiling Al' was prone to arrive on unofficial visits with a jeroboam of champagne. And that morning Kesselring's hopes rode exceedingly high, for Test Group 210 were charged to knock out four key radar stations—then known as R.D.F. (radio direction finding) stations—on the Kent and Sussex coasts. (A fifth at Ventnor on the Isle of Wight, had been assigned to fifteen JU 88s.)

Set down amid the apple orchards and the flat salt marshes that girdled the south coast, the brick-built stations, in tightly-guarded six-acre sites, were a mystery to all except the screened personnel who lived and worked there. Isolated units in a chain of twenty stations, that stretched from the Shetlands to the Isle of Wight, they were at all times markedly conspicuous through their sinister lattice-works of towers, steel towers rising 350 feet for the transmission aerials, wooden towers 240 feet high for the receivers. Already the sites had prompted a formidable crop of rumours. Along the coast, many countrymen swore that they were geared to cut out a hostile aircraft's engine at one flick of a switch.

The truth, if more prosaic, spelt equal danger to the Luftwaffe. Once the echo of an approaching aircraft showed as a V-shaped blip of light on the glass screen in the station's Receiver Block, the news passed within forty seconds along a formidable chain of command: by landline from the detector station to the Filter Room of Fighter Command, forty-two feet below ground at Stanmore, Middlesex, to the Ops Room next door, known mysteriously as 'Room 24', from thence to the Ops Rooms of Nos. 10, 11, and 12 Groups, and on to such sector stations as North Weald, Biggin Hill, Kenley, and Middle Wallop.

The entire labyrinthine structure of 'Stuffy' Dowding's Fighter Command stood or fell by this high-

above: Low towers of the RAF Chain Home radar defence system near Dover; left: A still from the 1968 film *Battle of Britain* depicting the radar plot room at RAF Fighter Command headquarters in the Battle of Britain; right: Assisting the pilot of an Me 110 day/night fighter before a mission in the summer of 1940.

pressure plotting, which from the first blip on a radar screen to a squadron's frantic "scramble" had a time lapse of exactly six minutes.

At nine a.m. on August 12, no one was later to recall any discernible sense of tension. In Fighter Command's Filter Room, the WAAF plotters, alerted through telephone headsets plugged into jack sockets in the table's edge, were readying their magnetic 'rakes' to position counters, coloured red, yellow and blue, representing Luftwaffe formations; every five minutes these would be changed, enabling the controller to see the 'age' of a plot. The atmosphere was much the same in that morning's target stations" Pevensey, hard by Eastbourne, Dover, Dunkirk, near Canterbury, and Rye, close to the old Kentish seaport.

Corporal Daphne Griffiths, one of the morning watch of four at Rye, who had just taken over the screen in the flimsy wooden Ops hut, was already, at nineteen, a veteran of the Receiver Block. Like all of her intake at Bawdsey Manor, on the Suffolk coast, Daphne had toiled through the long eight-hour watches, coped with time checks, plotted 'friendlies' up the Channel and already—she had to admit it—thought of Rye as 'home.'

As they settled to their tasks that morning, wholly absorbed in a system that each of them took entirely for granted, few realized that five years back, when most were teenagers, no such system had even existed.

On another historic Tuesday—February 26, 1935—four men were anxiously scanning the sky from a hummocky pasture at Weedon, Northamptonshire, four miles from the powerful Daventry radio transmitter which the BBC had erected in 1925. They were awaiting what one Fighter Command expert was later to call "the most critically-watched aircraft in the history of British aviation."

Heading the party was Robert (later Sir Robert) Watson-Watt, a plump forty-two-year-old Scot, Chief of the National Physical Laboratory's Radio Research Station at Slough, Buckinghamshire. Together with his junior scientific officer, Arnold 'Skip' Wilkins,, lean and laconic, their driver, Mr Dyer, and Albert P. Rowe, of the Air Ministry's Directorate of Scientific Research, Watson-Watt was on time for a rendezvous with a bomber.

The aircraft they awaited, a lumbering Heyford night bomber laid on by the Royal Aircraft Establishment at Farnborough, had been briefed to fly at 6,000 feet along a fixed track of twenty miles, up and down the Daventry fifty-metre beam. To the pilot, Squadron Leader Bobby Blucke, it was a totally boring assignment; he assumed, as he later allowed, it was 'some BBC job.'

When the first drone of the Heyford's engines became audible, the men, surprisingly, abandoned their vigil. All four hastily repaired inside a biscuit-coloured Morris caravan, to fix their eyes on the screen of a cathode-ray oscillograph, much like an ordinary television set. In the very centre of the screen, a bright green spot was glowing.

Steadily, the Heyford droned nearer. With equal steadiness, the green spot grew to an inch in length, then, as the engine throb receded, shrank once more. A moment passed, then Watson-Watt broke the silence. "Britain has become an island once more."

The demonstration, suggested by the prudent Air Vice Marshal Sir Hugh Dowding, then Air Member for Research and Development, had pointed the way to the brightest of futures: a £10,000 Treasury subsidy.

For fully three years, Britain's nakedness in the event of an air war had been a cause of grave

left: WAAFs on an RAF fighter staion in 1940; bottom left: Wing Commander Brendan 'Paddy' Finucane at RAF Hornchurch; below: Assistant Section Officer Edith Heap of the Women's Auxiliary Air Force, joined the WAAF in 1939 as an M.T. driver, later became a plotter and finally an intelligence officer debriefing bomber crews. Her fiancé, Pilot Officer Denis Wissler, one of The Few, was killed in action on 11 November 1940.

NEWS CHRONICLE
PLA E CHART, o. 2
GERMAN BOMBERS

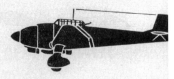

JUNKERS JU. 87

Single engine dive bomber. Wings are fi
with air-brakes for dive bombing. Inver
gull-wing, spatted non-retracting un
carriage, humpback appearance of the coc
cover. Note square fin and rudder.

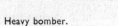

HEINKEL HE. III

Heavy bomber.
Dimensions: Span 73 ft. 10 in. Length 57 ft.
Two engines.
Fuselage is finely tapered. Wings are tape
sharply in front from the engine nacelles
tips. Tail-plane and elevators form elli
Latest types have long, transparent nose.

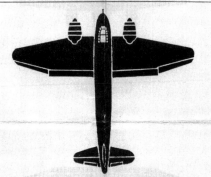

UNKERS JU. 88

Medium bomber. Wings are squarely taper
Has slim fuselage like Dornier Do. 17;
single fin and rudder. Most notice
feature is the engines which are Junk
inverted V 12s and not radials as they app
to be. They are fitted below the wings
project almost as far forward as the tip
the nose.

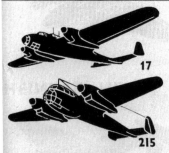

17

215

215

1

21

DORNIERS DO. 17 & 215

Medium bombers. The Do. 215 is the
proved version of the Do. 17 which bec
known as the "Flying Pencil" because of
very slender, tapering fuselage.
Dimensions: Span 59 ft. Length 55 f
Twin fins and rudders attached to tips of
plane and semi-circular wing tips are distinc
Nose of the Do. 215 is broader than Do.
The later type also has downward firing

concern to the prescient few. As far back as November 1932, a former and future Prime Minister, Stanley Baldwin, had gloomily written off Britain's chances of survival: "The bomber will always get through." On February 7, 1934, the Member for Epping, the Rt. Honourable Winston Churchill, although a loner in the political wilderness, had yet conjured up to the House of Commons, a vision of "the crash of bombs exploding in London . . . the cataracts of masonry and fire and smoke," concluding, "We are vulnerable as we have never been before." Four months later, a search by Albert Rowe of the Air Ministry's dusty files revealed only fifty-six that covered air defence.

"Unless science evolves some new method of aiding our defence, we are likely to lose the next war if it starts within ten years," he warned his chief, Harry Wimperis.

Wimperis, an urbane Scot, now turned to his old friend and fellow Scot, Watson-Watt: Was a Death Ray, then unknown outside the B-movie world of Boris Karloff, in any way feasible? The problem, passed for evaluation to Arnold Wilkins, came up against a blank wall: no aircraft would linger long enough in the most intense beam of radio energy the scientists could produce to knock out its engine. Watson-Watt: "well, I wonder what we can do to help them?"

Although Watson-Watt was later hailed as "the Father of British Radar," Wilkins, his chief always claimed, was "the Mother." It was Wilkins who had recalled how Post Office engineers so often complained that radio reception was disturbed when aircraft flew close to their receivers.

Then might not an aircraft's electro-magnetic energy be visually depicted by use of the cathode-ray apparatus? The pathway to Weedon had been charted.

Until this moment, Britain's resources had been primitive in the extreme. The sole detector system then centred on the Romney Mirror, a concave concrete block 200 feet long and twenty-five feet high, facing across the Channel on Romney Marsh in Kent. Given ideal conditions, the microphones dotted along its length could give rough bearings of an aircraft eight miles distant, but height and range were outside the Mirror's scope. Motor cars, boats, flights of birds, could make even bearings dubious. The Mirror's one back-up system was the 30,000 members of the Observer Corps—duly rechristened the Royal Observer Corps by 1941—who, equipped with binoculars, armbands and helmets, could spot planes only after they had crossed over the coast line, an arrangement which Churchill derided as 'Early Stone Age'.

After Weedon, events moved swiftly. On May 13, 1935, an RDF experimental unit under Watson-Watt, was set up on the Suffolk coast at Orfordness, equipped with a seventy-five-foot radio aerial. By September, Orfordness was tracking aircraft fifty eight miles away. Urged on by Wimperis, the Air Ministry invested £24,000 in acquiring nearby Bawdsey Manor from Sir Cuthbert Quilter, a telephone pioneer, whose family motto, appropriately, was FIRST IN THE FIELD. Bawdsey was now the focal point of a £100,000 project, the world's first radar station, soon capable of locating aircraft at a range of 150 miles, at heights of up to 30,000 feet.

It was, Wimperis noted in a memo to Dowding, a system "which will be independent of mist, cloud, fog or nightfall . . . at the same time . . . vastly more accurate than present methods."

By 1937, Bawdsey had become a magnet, attracting such scientific luminaries as Sir Henry Tizard, Chairman of the Committee for the Scientific Survey of Air Defence, Albert Rowe, who took over from Watson-Watt in 1938, and Professor Patrick Blackett, a Nobel Prize winner. Under their surveillance, the first of the Air Ministry Experimental Stations (AMES)—later called Chain Home Stations—were rising at twenty-five-mile intervals along the coastline of Britain. Bawdsey itself by May 1937, three

months after the first training school for radar ops was opened, Dover by July of that year, Canewdon, in Essex, by August. A dedicated community of fifty physicists, who dispensed with nine-to-five routines, the 'Bawdsey Soviets' talked radar from breakfast to bedtime, evolving the streamlines plotting techniques that were to become known as 'the Tizzy Angle.'

Inevitable, from March 1935 on, with the new Luftwaffe a reality, the Germans grew curious—and none more so than General Wolfgang Martini, Commanding General of German Signals and Radar. In May 1939, and again in August, Martini reactivated the giant airship LG 127 Graf Zeppelin, despatching her across the North Sea to Bawdsey. From Good Friday 1939, the day that Mussolini invaded Albania, the Chain Home link had begun a twenty-four-hour watch that would not cease until war's end—yet with the Zeppelin's radio receivers emitting nothing but static, the 'Tizzy Angle' remained an unplumbed mystery.

Were those tall towers the eyes of The Few? Their ears? Martini didn't know—but before the Luftwaffe launched *Adler Angriff*, the Attack of the Eagles, on August 13, a prelude to the German seaborne invasion of England, Rubensdörffer's task was to neutralize them for good and all.

At 9.25 a.m. on August 12, Daphne Griffiths, in the Receiver Block at Rye, was suddenly alerted. A V-shaped blip of light had registered off northern France. Promptly she reported, "Hello, Stanmore, I've a new track at thirty miles. Only three aircraft—I'll give you a plot." Abruptly, the thought crossed her mind: were other stations plotting the same planes? But the Filter Room reassured her, she alone had registered them. Could they please have a height?

Although height was one of the teething troubles many radar operators had yet to master—most pilots added an extra 5,000 feet to their estimates to avoid being 'bounced', Daphne reported confidently, "Height, 18,000." She noted, too, that the range was fast decreasing; if the planes continued on course, they would pass directly overhead. "Stanmore, is this track still unidentified? The Filter Room seemed unperturbed. The plot had been marked with an X, signifying doubtful, to be watched and investigated further.

As the steep chalk cliffs of Dover loomed ahead, Hauptmann Walter Rubensdörffer knew no doubts whatsoever, visibility over the Straits was good, and all were geared for action. "Achtung, No. 3 Staffel," he signalled into his microphone, "Dismissed for special mission. Good hunting!" Promptly

Oberleutnant Otto Hintze and his section swung east towards Dover. Oberleutnant Martin Lutz and his men streaked for Pevensey. Rubensdörffer himself set course for Dunkirk, near Canterbury. The towering aerials at Rye were thus the target for Oberleutnant Wilhelm Roessiger.

In Rye's Receiver Block, the station adjutant, Flying Officer Smith, now recalled that the Ops hut was protected only by a small rampart of sandbags. He told Corporal Sydney Hempson, the NCO in charge, "I think it would be a good idea if we had our tin hats." Simultaneously, the voice of Troop Sergeant Major Johnny Mason, whose Bofors guns defended the site, seemed to explode in their headsets: "Three dive-bombers coming out of the sun—duck!"

Mindful that this was the Glorious Twelfth, Assistant Section Officer Violet Hime, the WAAF administrative officer, muttered a dry aside, "They've mistaken us for grouse."

Still glued to her set, Daphne Griffiths heard a faint faraway voice in her headphones, barely audible above the snarling whine of Roessiger's engines: "Rye, what's happening? Why don't you answer me?" Still mortified that her plot had been relegated to an 'X', Daphne replied quite coldly, "Your 'X' raid is bombing us, Stanmore, and it's no wonder you can't hear me, we can't hear ourselves either!"

It seemed at first that Rubensdörffer's split-second timing had paid off. At Rye, the Ops hut shuddered convulsively; glass and wooden shutters toppled; chunks of chalk were blasted 400 feet high to bespatter the steel aerials. Beneath the table, Daphne and her fellow plotters, Helen McCormick and Brenda Hackett, watched chairs and tables spiralling above them, and the same confusion prevailed everywhere. At Pevensey, tons of gravel swamped the office of Flight Lieutenant Marcus Scroggie, the C.O., only minutes after he had left it. At Dunkirk, one Rubensdörffer bomb literally shifted the con-

left: A Spitfire pilot on the wing of his plane, believed to be at the Westhampnett satellite of Tangmere in 1940; right: The bomb aimer of a German aircraft during the Battle of Britain.

left: R.R. Stanford Tuck in his Hurricane; bottom left: A Heinkel He 111 as seen from the nose of another; below: The gun camera view of shooting down a twin-engined German aircraft; right: Residents of Ponder's End, Enfield, examining the wreckage of a Bf 110 Messerschmit shot down over their neighbourhood on 30 August 1940.

crete transmitter block by inches; at Dover, one of Hintze's bombs sheared past the recumbent operators to bury itself beneath the sick quarters. Yet in all instances, although the tall towers swayed palpably, they remained intact.

At Ventnor, on the Isle of Wight, it was a different story. Pounded by fifteen Junkers 88 dive-bombers, the station was swept by a curtain of fire, and the Fire Brigade, pumping up water through 560 yards, were barely able to cope. All this was narrated to Fighter Command's Filter Room in a frenzied running commentary from an NCO on site, who lamented repeatedly that a WAAF named 'Blondie' was missing. This was so stirring to Pilot Officer Robert Wright, Dowding's personal assistant and a

below: Refueling Hawker Hurricane fighters in 1940.

pre-war screenplay writer, that he shattered the Filter Room's cathedral calm by seizing a microphone and yelling "Well, where are the rest of you?"

At once a disdainful colleague reproved him, "Don't get too Hollywood," so infuriating Wright he forgot whose side he was on. "You English make me sick," he blazed back.

On the coast there was less excitement; most of the personnel were too stunned to react. At Rye, Violet Hime, groping shakily from the floor of the Ops hut, her eyes and nostrils choked with grit, found Corporal June Alderson, a striking blonde, diffidently proffering a cigarette. "I'll light it for you too, ma'am, if my hand isn't shaking too much." When Violet saw no trace of a tremor in the corporal's hand,

she knew a moment of pure triumph. Some days earlier, the camp's flight sergeant had enquired casually how soon RAF operators would be replacing the WAAF; if an invasion was imminent, a clutch of hysterical airwomen would badly affect morale. Within hours of the raid—which delivered forty bombs on Rye in exactly four minutes—he was back to offer abject apologies: "We're proud to have the WAAF on the station with us."

The Women's Auxiliary Air Force was formed on June 28th 1939, by Royal Warrant. At the outbreak of the Second World War on September 3rd 1939, there were less than 2,000 women on strength. Its object was to replace RAF men, where practicable, freeing them for other active service.

When war was declared, an appeal for recruits for the WAAF was broadcast by the BBC, and from all walks of life hundreds of women immediately volunteered. But to begin with, the WAAFs had very little uniform or equipment, inadequate acccommodation, little proper training, and no clear rules or traditions of their own. They had to contend with difficult, makeshift conditions during the severe first winter of the war, as well as with prejudice from some of the RAF who felt that women had no part to play in the Service, and that they would panic under bombardment.

The first recruits were given a choice of only five trades, as Cooks, Drivers MT, Equipment Assistants, Clerks, or Orderlies. But as the war progressed and the Service grew, this choice increased, until by 1943 there were twenty-two officer branches and seventy-five trades, with nearly 182,000 women employed. Without this participation by the WAAF, the RAF would have required 150,000 more men.

Working side by side with the RAF at home and overseas, throughout the war, the WAAF won many honours and awards, including six Military Medals for "Gallantry in the face of the enemy," and thousands of "Mentioned in Despatches."

The great majority, however, worked with no reward. Their hours were long, conditions sometimes harsh, their life dull and their duties unglamourous, whilst their work could be both dirty and dangerous.

They earned the full admiration and gratitude of the RAF, and the Air Council stated: "It is the view of the Air Council that an essential operational factor of the RAF would be missing if there was no WAAF." And a Group Captain in command of a front line fighter station during the Battle of Britain declared: "I had cause to thank goodness that this country could produce such a race of women as the WAAF on my station."

I am the daughter of Earth and Water, / And the nursling of the Sky; / I pass through the pores of the ocean and shores: / I change but I cannot die. / For after the rain when with never a stain / The pavilion of Heaven is bare, / And the winds and sunbeams with their convex gleams / Build up the blue dome of air, /I silently laugh at my own cenotaph, / And out of the caverns of rain, / Like a child from the womb, like a ghost from the tomb, / I arise and unbuild it again.
—from *The Cloud* by Percy Bysshe Shelley

At Calais-Marck airfield, Rubensdörffer and his team were quietly exultant; every squadron had scored triumphantly. Pevensey was already reported silent; at Rye, Roessiger had accurately reported ten hits, not realizing that he had demolished ten empty barracks and that the main installations had gone

left: WAAF Evelyn Clarke at Tangmere in the summer of 1940; right: WAAF Corporal Elspeth Henderson (on left) at Biggin Hill in Kent on 18 August 1940.

every station except Ventnor, inoperative for the next eleven days, was reported back on the air, operating with standby diesels. It now seemed unlikely that the radar stations could be silenced for more than a few hours at a time, and three days later, Goering made the same point to his Luftflotte commanders at Karinhall. "It is doubtful whether there is any point in continuing the attacks on radar sites, in view of the fact that not one of them attacked has so far been put out of operation."

In fact, only two more attacks were ever launched: at Rye once more, on August 15, as well as Dover and Foreness, and at Poling, on August 18, when ninety bombs so badly damaged the station that a mobile unit was brought in to fill the gap.

Even though the commanders-in-chief shrugged off this setback, the rank-and-file were far from content. As the then-Major Adolf Galland, commanding JG 26, was to complain, "We had no fighter control at tht time, and no way of knowing what the British were doing with their forces as each battle progressed." Radar, he grumbled, seemed to give the British "superbinoculars" that could see across the Channel.

With this verdict, 'Stuffy' Dowding fully and wholeheartedly concurred. "Where would we have been without RDF and all that went with it? We could never have maintained the vast number of standing patrols that would have been necessary if we had not had that magic sight." Given that Dowding began the Battle in August with exactly 708 serviceable aircraft and 1,434 battle-worthy pilots—half the complement of an average postwar airline—that conclusion was inescapable.

Almost twenty years after the Battle of Britain, in July 1959, the Duchess of Gloucester was to unveil a plaque in Bawdsey's Officers Mess that paid final tribute to those pioneering days. It was, perhaps inevitably, a masterpiece of British understatement. IN THE YEAR 1936 AT BAWDSEY MANOR ROBERT WATSON-WATT AND HIS TEAM OF SCIENTISTS DEVELOPED THE FIRST AIR DEFENCE RADAR WARNING STATION. THE RESULTS ACHIEVED BY THESE PIONEERS PLAYED A VITAL PART IN THE SUCCESSFUL OUTCOME OF THE BATTLE OF BRITAIN IN 1940.

Between 29 October 1925 and 31 December 1995, the Royal Observer Corps, a civil defence organization, operated in the United Kingdom. It was headquartered at RAF Bentley Priory, Stanmore, north of London, and was made up mostly of civilian volunteers serving in their spare time. In its later years, the ROC members were under the administrative control of RAF Strike Command. They wore an RAF-style uniform, were trained by a cadre of full-time professional officers under the command of the Commandant Royal Observer Corps. The organization eventually was known as the Observer Corps. It was set up originally to provide for the visual detection, identification, tracking, and reporting of aircraft over Britain and, in April 1941, was awarded the title Royal by King George VI in recognition of service carried out by Observer Corps personnel during the Battle of Britain.

left: Observer Corps volunteers monitoring an enemy air raid approaching in 1940; below: A German bomb aimer in a raid on a target in southern England during the Blitz

To produce the necessary conditions for the reduction of England ... I order the following:
The German Air Forces must with all means in their power and as quickly as possible destroy the English air force. The attacks must in the first instance be directed against flying formations, their ground organization, and their supply organizations, in the second against the aircraft production industry and the industries engaged in production of anti-aircraft equipment.

After achieving air superiority in terms of time and of area, the air war should be continued against harbours, especially those which are engaged in the provision of food supplies and also against the installations for food supplies in the heart of the country.
—Adolf Hitler, Directive No. 17, 1 August 1940

In a sense, the raid was symbolic of the Luftwaffe's entire conduct of the Battle. The timing was perfect—7.02 a..m. on Tuesday, August 13—and caught everyone unawares, as a good raid should. "Raid 45 is bombing Eastchurch drome," intoned the Bromley Observer Corps' controller, Brian Binyon, at the moment that fifty bomb-aimers of Bomber Group 2 bent to the five complex readings of their sights. Across the airfield, reactions were traumatic, which again was exemplary. In the NCO's quarters, Sergeant Reginald Gretton, of No. 266 Squadron, a devotee of the mess' shepherd's pie, cried out shrilly: "They're dropping bombs. They're dropping bombs on us!" Eastchurch, a haven of good home cooking, was suddenly and unforgivably in the front line. The commanding officer, Group Captain Frank Hopps, was more prosaic. "My God, this station's worth millions—some accountant's got a job to do writing off this lot."

There was formidable devastation—precisely what Oberst Johannes Fink, the bomber commander, would have wished. Five Bristol Blenheim night fighters were written off, plus twelve Spitfires of No. 266 Squadron, which were on overnight transit to Hornchurch. The Operations Block was untenable, all electricity and telephone lines had been severed, and vital petrol supplies destroyed. Yet Sergeant Gretton's surprise was wholly legitimate. Eastchurch was a Coastal Command station, whose patrols kept watch for German raiders over the North Sea. It was in no way part of the Fighter Command network that must be neutralized prior to Operation Sealion.

Later that same day, the Luftwaffe scored again—one of the few occasions in the Battle where the overrated Stuka dive-bombers triumphed. At 4 p.m., the teabreak, eighty-six of them achieved total surprise at Detling airfield near Maidstone, Kent, wrecking the runway, torching the hangars, demolishing the Ops Block, destroying twenty aircraft on the ground and claiming fifty lives—so bloodily that a local undertaker, Wallace Beale, needed only the five-foot coffins reserved for unidentified remains. For almost a day, Detling was non-operational, but this, too, was a Coastal Command airfield, where Dowding's writ did not run.

Yet one day earlier at Manston, Kent, Fighter Command's 530-acre forward base, code-named Charlie Three, the bomb-laden ME 109s and ME 110s of Hauptmann Rubensdörffer's Test Group 210 had achieved a victory—more decisive by far than the inconclusive raid on the radar stations. As Rubensdörffer's pilots peeled off in their dives, the Spitfires of No. 65 Squadron, caught at the second of take-off, were powerless to act, taxiing blindly through clouds of choking smoke. Overhead, Flight Lieutenant Al Deere, on that day leading No. 54 Squadron, was equally nonplussed by "a cloud like white pumice rising over the drome ... it was like a shroud over everything." Not realizing that it was chalk dust swirling from more than 100 craters, Deere thought that Manston was on fire. Flying

above: A German reconnaissance photo after a raid on an oil storage tank farm in the Thames Estuary; left: Heinkel bombers departing on a raid in summer 1940.

Officer Duncan Smith, of No. 600 Squadron, returning from leave in an old Tiger Moth biplane, was also flummoxed as he circled the drome, pondering, "Who's been spreading fertilizer?"

An all-grass field, lacking runways, Manston was in many ways an anachronism, a base dating back to 1916, when Germany's frontier had been the Rhine. Manned by a largely civilian staff, who kept strictly peacetime hours, Manston was still a station where things were done by the book: hard-pressed mechanics seeking a spanner, remembered Flight Sergeant John Wright, of 600 Squadron, "had to produce the right form at Main Stores—or else." The pilots of 32 Squadron had similarly bitter memories. On one occasion, refused transport to the mess because they lacked a form 658, they had commandeered a tractor at gunpoint—only to find that the chef had gone home and locked up the food. "The station was deeply resentful when I shot the lock off the larder," related Squadron Leader John Worrall. "but we ate."

Thus, at Manston, not surprisingly, nerves broke early and stayed broken; the civilian stance was all too infectious. On August 12, the airfield was at once a thundering horde of blue-clad men seeking shelter, bound for the deep chalk caves that wound like catacombs beneath the drome. Here hundreds, despite their officers' exhortations, were to stay for days on end, contracting out of the battle for the duration.

Attacks like these made total sense to fighter commanders like Adolf Galland. "The enemy air force must be wiped out while still grounded," he emphasized, following the tenet of the Italian General Giulio Douhet, the bombers' champion, for what Galland envisaged was the clinical elimination, one by one, of Fighter Command's airfields. But soon it was plain that the Luftwaffe's *Abteilung* 5, the intelligence arm, directed by a mere major, Josef 'Beppo' Schmid, made no distinction between Fighter-Command's airfields and others in southern England. Nor had Schmid, a non-operational officer who spoke no foreign language, had any liaison with General Wenniger, Germany's air attaché in London until the spring of 1939.

Were the radar stations vital or were they not? Which of Fighter Command's airfields most merited attack, and when attacking them, which targets mattered most—the hangars and buildings or planes on the ground? None of these questions had been adequately studied or thought through by Schmid and his staff.

Another forward base, Hawkinge, inland from Folkstone, was so scientifically pounded by Junkers 88 bombers on August 12 that it closed down for the rest of the day. Yet on August 15, when another attack, this time by Stukas, put Hawkinge out of action for two more days, other mass attacks were directed at secondary targets: once more at Eastchurch, and at the Short Brothers Aircraft factory at Rochester, Kent, whose final assembly line was producing not fighters but Britain's first four-engined bomber, the then massive Stirling. Within this timespan, the naval air stations at Gosport, Ford and Lee-on-Solent were hit as if the fate of Fighter Command depended on them. Had the Luftwaffe struck at every Fighter Command base as consistently as at Manston, Sealion might have been closer to fruition. On August 18, two squadrons of Test Group 210 harassed them yet again, though this time an unexpected resistance greeted the invaders; angered by the craven conduct of those skulking below ground, the officers and men of No. 600 Squadron had been working overtime. A Bristol Blenheim night fighter squadron, grounded by day, they had banded together, regardless of rank, to fill the gap—contriving such primitive armament as 'The Sheep Dipper', a spare set of Browning machine-guns rigged on a pole, and 'The Armadillo', a truck converted with concrete facings to a rudi-

mentary armoured car with a machine-gun fixed amidships. Now, as sixteen ME 110s launched the second all-out attack, a withering curtain of gunfire arose to meet them.

Crouched on an improvised fire-step of trestles, Pilot Officer Henry Jacobs was one of the six squadron air gunners determined to hit back against the Germans. As the swooping 110s shrank to slim pencils in their gunsights, fire from 'The Sheep Dipper's' dismantled Brownings went hammering up the sloping roof of No. 600 Squadron's crew room. Then, as the 500-pounders came whistling, blast tore all six gunners from the trestle in a blasphemous tangle of arms and legs.

It was a short-lived resistance, even so; within six days, morale at Manston was at lowest ebb. To the pilots of 266 Squadron, operational flights from Charlie Three spelt frustration from the first; the first devastating Eastchurch raid had cost them their Mae Wests and parachutes, and at Manston no storeman had come on duty to replace them. One flight commander, Flight Lieutenant Dennis Armitage, spent a murky half-hour groping through the labyrinth of caves, vainly seeking the station electrician he had entrusted to do a job. Finally, emerging into the strong sunlight, Armitage completed the job himself.

Across 500 deserted acres every officer could tell the same story. At 600 Squadron's dispersal, Pilot Officer Jacobs found it hard to repress his laughter; the station's accounts officer had wandered disconsolately by yet again, weighed down by two bags of silver. Although it was Sunday, he sought in vain

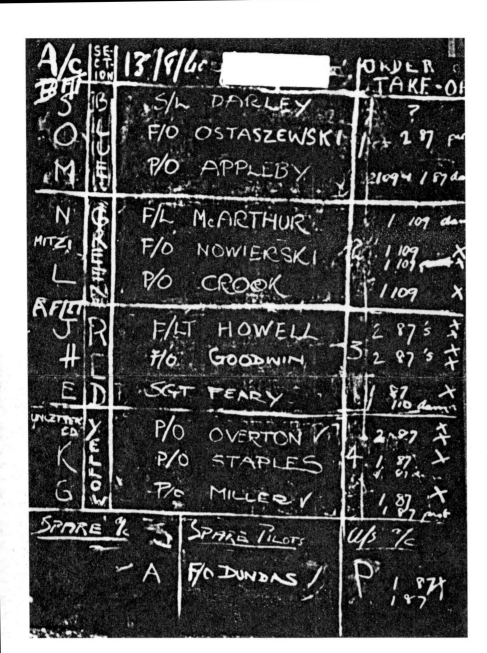

left: The 'state board' of 609 Squadron at RAF Middle Wallop for 13 August 1940; right: Ground personnel fuel a Heinkel He 111 bomber for raid on England.

enough airmen above ground to organize a pay parade.

By August 18, four all-out raids had ensured that few buildings were even habitable. With all water cut off, men shaved—if they shaved at all—at the pre-war swimming pool. Many were overwrought to the point of collapse. Only in the nick of time did Squadron Leader James Leathart, of No. 54 Squadron, stop a technical officer firing blind down a shelter to flush out the deserters, and Manston's chaplain, the Reverend Cecil King, acted as promptly. When an officer burst into the mess, brandishing a revolver, threatening to finish off himself and every man present, King led him gently from the

room, keeping up an anodyne flow of pleasantries until the man broke down, surrendering his gun. By now the end was very near. "Manston was literally taken from us piece by piece," recalled Henry Jacobs bitterly, for it had needed more than the brave archaic armament of No. 600 Squadron to stop the Luftwaffe. On August 18, when more ME 110s burst from the sun, Flying Officer David Clarkson and six others dived beneath the mess billiard table, emerging to find that bullets had sheared the baize from the slate, as cleanly as a knife might have done. All of them believed then that the Germans had meant to do it, and were engulfed with a sense of powerlessness.

There were more vital airfields for the Luftwaffe to tackle—but again on the haphazard basis of a chance spin of the coin. At lunchtime on August 18, thirty-one Dorniers of Oberstleutnant Fröhlich's Bomber Group 76 were assigned, by sheer chance, to strafe two of Fighter Command's most vital sector stations, covering the southern approaches to London—Kenley in Surrey, and Biggin Hill in Kent. Further to fox the radar stations, a spearhead of five Dorniers was to fly at wave-top height, homing in on both stations at nought feet, in precise concert with the high-level raids.

This now became a split-second decision for Kenley's controller, Squadron Leader Anthony Norman, although the Observer Corps had spotted the low level Dorniers, heading for the white chalk

left: The pilot of a Heinkel bomber on a raid to a British target; above: Sergeant George Unwin with 19 Squadron at RAF Duxford, near Cambridge.

quarry that marked out Kenley. HQ 11 Group had ordered no "scramble." So Norman acted on his own initiative. "Get them into their battle bowlers ... tin hats everybody," he ordered the floor supervisor, then, to Squadron Leader Aeneas MacDonell's 64 Spitfire Squadron: "Freema Squadron, scramble, patrol base, angels twenty."

Over Kenley, 64 Squadron were at first at a loss, until MacDonell's voice, high-pitched with urgency, ordered "Freema Squadron, going down." Sergeant Peter Hawke remembered thinking, 'Why down? We need all the height we can get,' until he saw the black corona of smoke pulsing from Kenley's hangars: the low level raid had arrived in advance of the high level strike. Seeing a flash like exploding

helium from a Dornier, Hawke recalled: "I just felt, my God! Did I do that? Then I thought, well, this was what I was trained to do."

Fifty feet above the airfield, the Hurricanes of Squadron Leader John Thompson's No. 111 Squadron, scrambled from nearby Croydon, were almost casualties themselves. No one had warned them that the station defences were firing parachute-and-cable rockets at the raiders—electrically fired rockets snaking upwards a forty feet a second to grapple the wings with steel wire. Now, Thompson thought in anguish, if one of those hits us we're finished.

For this risky exploit, Bomber Group 76 paid dearly: fully six Dorniers and their crews, and four of the JU 88 bombers that had accompanied them. But in their turn they had scored with painful accuracy. Ten hangars had been shattered, and six more damaged; the Ops Room was out of action and

The pilots of the Air Transport Auxiliary in the Second World War worked with the RAF ferry pools delivering military aircraft from the British factories, mostly to maintenance units for the installation of guns and accessories. Lord Beaverbrook, Minister for Aircraft Production: "The ATA ... carried out the delivery of aircraft from the factories to the RAF, thus relieving countless numbers of RAF pilots for duty in the Battle. They were soldiers fighting in the struggle just as completely as if they had been engaged on the battlfront."

many buildings had been reduced to trembling shells. Only one factor had saved Kenley from total destruction: many bombs from the low level raid had landed horizontally and they had failed to explode.

At Biggin Hill, the bulk of the 500 bombs dropped had landed wide, on the airfield's eastern perimeter, but the CO, Group Captain Richard Grice, still paraded the station personnel to issue a timely warning: "What happened at Kenley today can well happen here, so don't think that you've escaped." WAAFs like Corporal Elspeth Henderson recalled standing consciously taller: already their shoulders were bruised and aching after compulsory hours on the range with Lee-Enfield rifles, and now they were truly in the front line.

At Fighter Command, Dowding's personal assistant, Pilot Officer Robert Wright, recalled widespread consternation: did the Germans plan to concentrate the might of their bombers against the sector stations? In truth, as General Paul Deichmann, the Chief of Staff to the 2nd Flying Corps, was later to record, this fear was groundless. Never at any time did the Luftwaffe High Command suspect that Kenley and Biggin Hill—or, for that matter, Hornchurch, Tangmere and Middle Wallop—were sector stations, the nerve centres of Dowding's command. "We all thought priority command posts would be sited underground, away from the centre of operations, not in unprotected buildings in the centre of the airfields. And not all of them had sandbags or blast walls!"

Incredibly, Major Schmid had no liaison officers either with the fighter groups in the Pas de Calais or the bomber groups centred on Brittany; given this mix of ignorance and random planning, Manston was still seen as as good a target as any. By August 24, all efforts to hold it had proved in vain. As twenty JU dive-bombers, with a fighter escort, swept in over the drome, Pilot Officer Henry Jacobs, relaying a blow-by-blow commentary to HQ 11 Group, heard a hollow note like a gong echo up the wire; a bomb, striking the telephone and teleprinter links, had severed 248 circuits in one blow. Dashing from 600 Squadron's Ops Room, Jacobs saw the East Camp guardhouse had now vanished, swallowed into a chalky crater forty feet deep.

Fire swept all those buildings still standing, and Leading Fireman Herbert Evans, of Margate Fire Brigade, arriving on a motorcycle as the spearhead of the main fire force, never forgot the spectacle that met his eyes—"I was appalled at the damage done. The hangars were ablaze, planes on the field were blazing and in pieces ... there was not a soul to be seen except an RAF officer who stood gazing at the scene, pipe in mouth and hands in pockets, with tears streaming down his face. On seeing

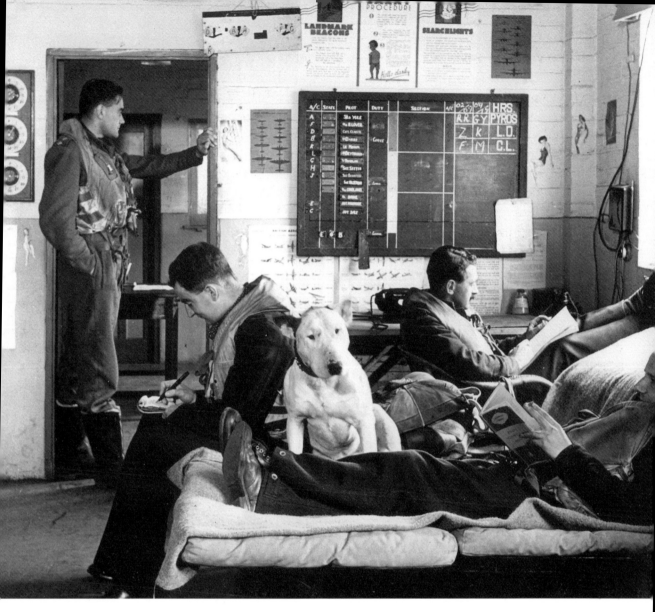

far left: A Royal Mail stamp issued to commemorate the award of the Distinguished Flying Cross; left: None less than the famous, high-achieving Johnnie Johnson said of Canadian Stan Turner (left): "... a fearless and great leader of his squadron"; above: A wonderful study of RAF fighter pilots in their crew room at dispersal, awaiting the call to go after the Hun.

me, he turned away and I never saw him again."

On the same day, the bulk of the station personnel were moved out, while Flight Sergeant John Wright hastily filled a 600 Squadron truck to overflowing with spare parts. Already civilians were moving in to loot tools and live ammunition from the main store: the shame of Manston was complete.

At Fighter Command, there was growing concern: would the panic prove contagious? Aircraftman Thomas MacKay recalled how at Hawkinge "it was so bad some boys took their blankets out and slept under the hedges . . . some were in such a state of nerves they didn't come back but stayed away all the time." At length, NCOs armed with revolvers were sent to flush them out like beaters at a shoot. At North Weald, too, the first bombs of August 24, saw men surging like frightened sheep from the main gates, bound for the glades of Epping Forest, until the powerful brogue of Wing Commander

right: A WAAF radio technician at work on a Spitfire in 1940; far right: A still from the 1968 film *Battle of Britain*;

98

Victor Beamish, the Irish CO boomed out through the Tannoy loudspeaker: "Any officer, NCO, or airman who leaves his post on duty is a coward and a rat—and I shoot rats on sight." There was no further panic at North Weald.

And for the most part calm did prevail. Edward R. Murrow, the CBS commentator, painted a graphic word picture of WAAFs coming on duty at Kenley a few hours after the raid of August 18—"Most of them were girls with blond hair and plenty of makeup. They marched well, right arms thrust forward and snapped smartly down, after the fashion of the Guards . . . Some of them were probably frightened, but every head was up . . . most of them were smiling." At many airfields, which underwent random bombing, like Warmwell, Dorset, the personnel viewed the vast German onslaught almost with detachment—"Have you ever seen anything so cool, so damned cool." Aircraftman Lawrence

James remembered applauding from a slit trench, "What efficient bastards they are!"

Some survivors believed that the airfield attacks brought about a new sense of cohesion. "At first the airmen hated us for wearing their uniform," said Rosemary Inness, a WAAF plotter at North Weald, "and the Chief Controller removed all WAAF from the Operations Room when unidentifiable plots appeared on the board, but finally, when the Ops Room received a direct hit, he so appreciated his WAAF who remained steadfastly plotting away with their tin hats on over their headsets that he allowed us special passes."

Towards August's end, there was need for such cohesion at all the fighter airfields. At first, 'The Few' in the sky had monopolized all the glory: now heroes and heroines became commonplace on the ground. When nine Junkers 88 dive-bombers streaked for Biggin Hill on August 30, cutting off all electricity, water and gas, killing or injuring sixty-five, more than forty WAAFs sheltering in a trench were engulfed by tons of chalk and stones, but some were on duty the next day—still chuckling at the WAAF Flight Sergeant Gartside's outraged complaint: "My God, they've broken my neck—and they've broken my false teeth too!" Among them was Corporal Elspeth Henderson, who worked on next day until a 500-pound bomb from a second raid tore through the Ops Room roof—one of only six WAAFs to be awarded the Military Medal during the entire war.

Now the main London-Westerham telephone cable connecting Biggin Hill with the outside world was severed: the onus lay on Hornchurch Sector Station, covering the Thames Estuary, to control Biggin's squadrons and satellites, Gravesend and Redhill, as well as its own, Rochford. Six squadrons were to be manoeuvred in combat over 5,000 square miles of sky—and on August 30, Hornchurch too, was decisively blitzed.

At 1.15 p.m., Wing Commander Cecil Bouchier had been first on the scene, to find more than 100 craters pitting what he saw as his airfield. Promptly, all leave passes were cancelled and Bouchier himself led the working parties filling in the holes with pick and shovel, placing yellow cardboard cones to mark the sites of unexploded bombs. Pilot Officer Henry Jacobs remembered: "Whatever your rank, you were in there pitching." Jacobs had moved up from Manston with 600 Squadron, and aircraftman George Stokes, Al Deere's cherished flight mechanic, recalled the spirit of those times. "The CO put out an appeal for all nearby civilians to help. They came in their dozens with spades and shovels . . . they worked so hard that everything was back to normal in four hours."

But could even such concerted teamwork prevail against a determined Luftwaffe? After numerous false starts they were learning to strike hard where it counted most, so that even the most sanguine of pilots had cause to wonder. On September 1, raid followed raid with the deadly precision of a hammer driving home nails: Hawkinge, Detling, Lympne, Biggin Hill, then Debden, Rochford, North Weald and Biggin yet again. And at Warmwell, Flight Lieutenant David Crook, of 609 Squadron, recalled the Duke of Wellington's words at Waterloo: "Hard pounding this, gentlemen: let's see who will pound longest."

Their deliverance, when it came, surprised nobody more than the Imperial General Staff. On the afternoon of Saturday, September 7, a meeting called by their chief, General Sir John Dill, was just under way when Brigadier Leslie Hollis entered with a message. Dill, after studying it anxiously, still recognized that 4 p.m. was the hour of Winston Churchill's catnap. "I think we should inform the Prime Minister," he said.

"Will he be awake yet?"

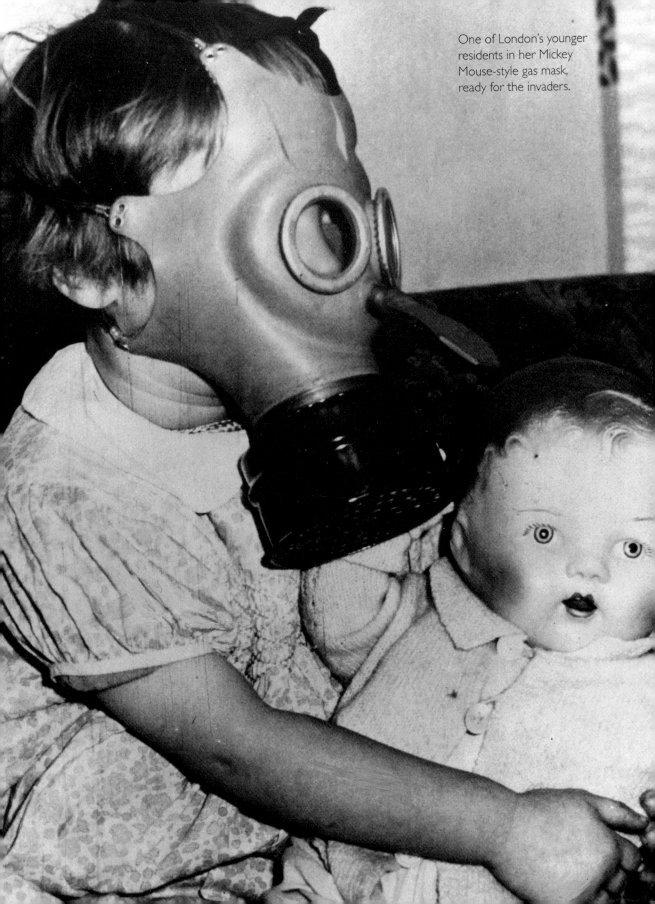

One of London's younger
residents in her Mickey
Mouse-style gas mask,
ready for the invaders.

below: Sergeant Pilot Denis Robinson of 152 Squadron at Warmwell, Dorset, survived this crash of his Spitfire near Wareham on 8 August 1940; right: Boulton-Paul Defiants of No. 264 Squadron, Kirton-in-Lindsay. These extremely vulnerable turret fighters proved utterly unsuited for their role and were ultimately relegated to a night-fighter assignment.

Even in the weekend silence of Whitehall, the sound of explosions could be clearly heard. "If he wasn't before, he is now," Hollis replied. "I'll go and tell him that they're bombing London."

"I believe this plan (raiding RAF airfields and British aircraft factories) would have been successful, but as a result of the Führer's speech about retribution, in which he asked that London be attacked immediately, I had to follow the other course. I wanted to interpret the Führer's speech about attacking London in this way. I wanted to attack the airfields first, thus creating a prerequisite for attacking London ... I spoke to the Führer about my plans in order to try to have him agree I should attack the first ring of RAF airfields around London, but he insisted he wanted to have London itself attacked for political reasons, and also for retribution. I considered the attacks on London useless, and I told the Führer again and again that inasmuch as I knew the English people as well as I did my own people, I could never force them to their knees by attacking London. We might be able to subdue the Dutch people by such measures but not the British."
—Hermann Goering at the International Military Tribunal, Nuremberg, 1946

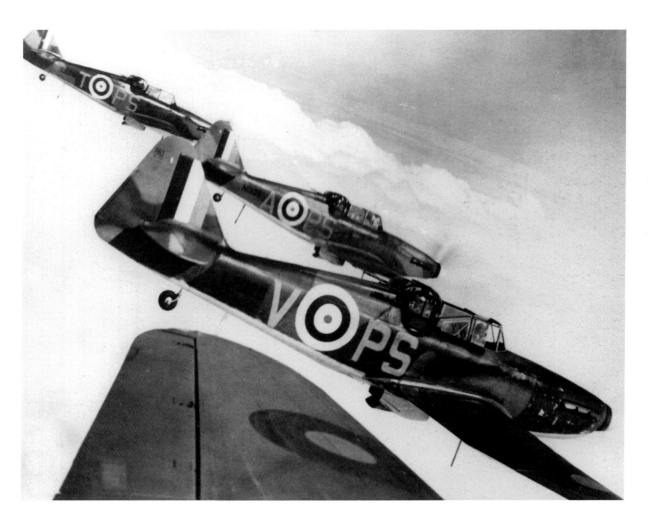

Scramble!

Afterwards, when they looked back to that summer, the scene was archetypal. A dozen or more pilots would be mustered at dispersal, overtly relaxed in deck-chairs, and on canvas cots, or stretched out on the cool grass. They wore flying overalls, sometimes pulled on hastily over pyjamas, or rolltop sweaters if the day was chilly. Almost all had silk scarves for comfort: in combat the neck would swivel constantly. These men were at Readiness, with Mae Wests—lifejackets—duly adjusted. Those on standby, were already in their cockpits, facing the wind, engines ready to turn over. Only the fortunate few had drawn Available status, with twenty minutes leeway before they took off.

Conversation was essentially sporadic. A few, like No. 603 Squadron, at Hornchurch, kept the demons at bay with Mah-Jong, a Chinese game played with chips and bamboo counters, or darts or shove ha'penny. Others leafed through magazines—*Illustrated*, *Picture Post*—or checked on Jane's state of undress in the current *Daily Mirror*. Only the ground crews rooted on terra firma, could concentrate on paperbacks; at Biggin Hill, Aircraftman Harold Mead was engrossed in the pulp thriller *No Orchids for Miss Blandish*, while one Debden flight sergeant gave his mechanics a crash course in *Lady Chatterley's Lover*. Music, too, was a potent aid to distraction; *Sweet Violetta* for 603 at Hornchurch, Dorothy Lamour's *These Foolish Things*, revolving endlessly on a tinny gramophone for 66 at Kenley. Only later would it be time for ribald ditties—*Bang Away Lulu*, *O'Riley's Daughter*, *The Ball o'Kirriemuir*—thumped out on the mess piano at night. These were survivors' songs, songs for the fortunate who had lived through the day's scrambles.

Pilot Officer Geoffrey Page of No. 56 Squadron, would recreate one of those scrambles with almost total recall, even to the date and the time—5.20 p.m. on August 12—and for the best of reasons: it was a scramble that almost cost him his life, and was to involve nineteen operations on atrociously burned face and hands. Thus he remembered that the scramble took place at Rochford airfield, the old Southend Flying Club, the satellite for North Weald sector station. At Rochford, as at most satellites, chairs and tables were unknown luxuries. Apart from a large bell tent, the one item of furniture was the field telephone, linking No. 56 to North Weald" the Scramble telephone.

The sounds of that day were largely subliminal. No one any longer heard the thump-thump of the petrol bowser's delivery pumps dinning in their ears. But Page remembered quite vividly the screeching brake drums of the wagon that delivered the heavy Thermos flasks of tea, the hunks of cut bread-and-butter, the communal jar of strawberry jam. It was in the midst of a childish game with the jam, poising a spoonful above a crawling wasp, that Page had felt his hand tremble violently, and seen the jam spill wide. The telephone rang, and his flight commander, Flight Lieutenant E.J. 'Jumbo' Gracie had lunged for it, before struggling to his feet: "Scramble . . . seventy-plus approaching Manston . . . angels one-five."

Then, as always, Page felt the sense of sickness drain away. As he sprinted the fifty yards to his waiting Hurricane, neatly inscribed 'Little Willie.' his mind was growing clear and alert. His right foot slipped into the stirrup step, his left foot gained the port wing. One short move then brought his right foot to the step inset in the fuselage. Now he was secure in the cockpit, and his rigger was deftly passing the parachute straps across his shoulders, then the Sutton harness straps. His mask was clipped across and oxygen switched on.

Then Page had primed the engine, adjusting the switches, and now his thumbs went up to signal to the mechanics. The chocks slipped away, the Rolls-Royce Merlin engines roared into life, and now No. 56 Squadron was heading for Manston, otherwise Charlie Three, the dancing grass flattening

left: Bob Doe was a fourteen-victory ace in the Battle of Britain; right: Geoffrey Page was credited with seventeen kills in his wartime career, was horribly burnt when his Hurricane was shot down on 12 August 1940, and was a founding member and first chairman of the Guinea Pig Club at the East Grinstead cottage hospital.

beneath the slipstreams.

Now, in this classic scramble, the voice of Wing Commander John Cherry, the North Weal controller, was filling their earphones: "Hullo, Yorker Blue Leader, Lumba calling. Seventy-plus bandits approaching Charlie Three, angels one-five." At once Gracie's voice acknowledged: "Hullo, Lumba, Yorker Blue Leader answering. Your message received and understood. Over."

About 100 miles southwest, over Warmwell airfield in Dorset, Pilot Officer Eugene 'Red' Tobin, one of the American pilots serving with No. 609 Squadron, heard an equally bizarre ukase from Squadron Leader Gavin Anderson, controlling Middle Wallop sector: "Hullo, Sorbo Leader, this is Bandy. Patrol Portland angels twenty. Many many bandits." As a typical pilot, Tobin's mind responded automatically: Is my manifold pressure too high? Will the guns work? Is the oil pressure dropping?

Yet was there truly such a thing as a typical pilot? All told, some 1,434 of them would be airborne some time after August 8, from the sensitive twenty-year-old Page, who had contended with fear all his life, to the deveil-may-care Red Tobin, a twenty-three-year-old real estate operator's son from Los Angeles. On the surface, these two had little in common, yet like most of 'Dowding's chicks', they and the others shared one attribute: an intense individuality. Few were aces, in the Tuck-Bader-Malan tradition, but all of them in the phrasing of a later generation, "did their own thing." This alone was the common bond uniting a fraternity as diverse as Rodolphe, Comte de Grune, a Belgian Condor Legion veteran, now fighting against his onetime allies with the pilots of 32 Squadron, and Squadron Leader Aeneas MacDonnell, official head of the Glengarry Clan; that linked Derek Boitel-Gill, the Nazam of Hyderabad's former personal pilot with Randy Matheson, the ex-Argentine gaucho, Jimmy Bryson, the Canadian Mountie, and Hugh Percy of No. 264 Squadron, a former Cambridge undergraduate who kept his log book in Greek.

Battle of France and Battle of Britain veteran Brian Kingcome, in the Spitfire cockpit, commanded 92 Squadron at Biggin Hill in Kent.

Air Chief Marshal Sir Hugh Dowding, on the ethics of shooting at aircraft crews who have baled out in parachutes: "Germans descending over England are prospective prisoners of war and, as such, should be immune. On the other hand, British pilots descending over England are still potential combatants. Much indignation was caused by the fact that German pilots sometimes fired on our descending airmen (although in my opinion they were perfectly entitled to do so), but I am glad to say that in many cases they refrained and sometimes greeted a helpless adversary with a cheerful wave of the hand."

Sergeant John Burgess flew Spitfires with 222 Squadron at Hornchurch in the Battle of Britain.

Fully fourteen squadrons were made up of auxiliaries, wealthy weekend fliers who defied all conventions on principle. Thus, Flight Lieutenant Sir Archibald Hope's 601 (County of London) Squadron at Tangmere, sported scarlet silk linings to their uniforms because the RAF's powder blue depressed them; a poker game with 601 was usually £100 a stake. Before No. 602 (City of Glasgow) Squadron accepted 'Sandy' Johnstone as their CO, they plied him with enough liquor to fell a lesser man: a gentleman must be able to hold his drink. When 'Big Jim' McComb's No. 611 (West Lancashire) Squadron approached an airfield, they flew, as a perverse tradition of their own, in perfectly defined swastika formation.

All through the battle, a behind-the-scenes army had backed their endeavours from the first: the riggers, fitters, flight mechanics, instrument repairers and armourers, were known generically as the 'ground crews'. "We lived rough and ready," said Corporal Ernest Wilson, who saw service with No. 17 (Hurricane) Squadron at Debden, and Leading Aircraftman Eric Marsden, a veteran of No. 145 Squadron at the Tangmere satellite, Westhampnett, supplies unpalatable detail: "There were no beds for us ... I made my bed from a couple of hedge stakes which I laid on some bricks which I scrounged and I used a Hurricane rigging mat." Many had worked under such conditions since June 24, when the squadrons Dowding withheld from France had been converted from two-pitch to constant-speed (variable pitch) propellers for maximum take-off and flight speed. To ensure the changeover, the mechanics had worked all night in blacked-out hangars, making do on ten-minute coffee breaks.

Far from being automatons, they too were individuals, used to doing their own thing. Following the example of Flying Officer Robert Lucy, No. 54 Squadron's engineer officer, they improvised. On one occasion, Lucy wrenched some armour plating from the seatback of one written-off Spitfire, coaxed a Hornchurch garage to fashion it into two stout fishplates and used them to patch another Spitfire's badly-holed starboard wing root. "I took the fairing off each night to make sure it was bearing the strain, but it was still flying in October." In this same tradition, Aircraftman Harold Mead, faced with an eighteen-inch gash in a Spitfire's wing, cut a slice from a petrol can and tacked it into place with four rivets. Time, the ground crews knew, was always of the essence. At Duxford, LAC William Eslick and his crew once saved themselves precious minutes by switching the access point to the compressed air bottles powering the guns—from an inaccessbile trap in the cockpit floor to a point behind the pilot's seat, with easier access through the sliding hood.

As LAC Eric Marsden recalled it, theirs was a lonely life—"Parochial is about the best way to describe the whole set-up ... we didn't mix ... the people in B Flight didn't know the people in A Flight. We lived a very narrow existence." It could be a fraught existence too, as when B Flight's commander, Adrian Boyd, once returned to Tangmere seething with anger: the 'enemy aircraft' he had been chasing all over France ... turned out to be specks in the bottom of the windscreen. Marsden: "In no short order, we got cleaning rags and perspex polish after that, so we were able to keep things absolutely top line."

On some of the outlying stations, the mechanics—after consultation with their pilots—mocked up the legends that adorned the planes, legends that laid stress on the don't-give-a-damn spirit. Many were Disney-oriented. Big Jim McComb's Spitfire, operational from the Duxford satellite, Fowlmere, from September 11, had Snow White on its fuselage; other 611 men, according to temperament, were Grumpy, Sneezy, and Dopey. Hurricane pilot Ian Gleed, of 87 Squadron, based at Exeter, had Figaro, with the diminuitive cat swatting a swastika, as blithely as a mouse. Willie McKnight, of Douglas Bader's

No. 242 Squadron, had a sharp-edged scythe dripping blood, to symbolize death, the grim reaper. The Fleet Air Arm's Sub-Lieutenant Jimmie Gardner—one of sixty-eight Fleet Air Arm pilots on loan to the RAF, and slow to discard their starched white collars—had 'England Expects', but spelt out in flags, to affirm his naval status.

Few men tilted so irreverently as Flying Officer D.H. Ward of No. 87 Squadron, a New Zealander who did not survive the Battle: his Hurricane coat-of-arms was made up from a figure 13, a broken mirror, a man on a ladder, and three on a match, captioned, 'So what the hell?'

In support of the pilots who made the scrambles, were the station commanders who turned the blindest of eyes to protocol and red tape. At Biggin Hill, Group Captain Richard Grice laid on crates of beer for all pilots returning from a day's last sortie; on one occasion, when Sergeant Ronnie Hamlyn, 610 Squadron, was three times scrambled during a disciplinary hearing, Grice finally met him at dispersal to "officially admonish" him for a careless landing. (That day's toll of five victims earned for Hamlyn the Distinguished Flying Medal). North Weald's CO, Victor Beamish, would leap through his office window rather than miss a scramble. At Northolt, Group Captain Stanley Vincent's Station Defence Flight—a lone Hurricane—had been formed to get him airborne whenever possible.

By common concensus, the doyen of station commanders was Wing Commander Cecil Bouchier, the bright, peppery CO of Hornchurch, who kept morale at peak with non-stop commentaries on the Ops Room's Tannoy loudspeakers. At mealtimes in the officer's mess, Old Sam, the chef, with his tall white cap, kept up his soothing flow of patter at Bouchier's behest. "Don't say you can't touch a bite, sir . . . just a shaving of the roast beef now . . . some of the underdone." At night, Bouchier even dispensed with electricity, importing candles from Harrods' at his own expense, a softer light for the taut, strained boyish faces. "You always tried to wear your best blue for 'Daddy' Bouchier's candlelight dinners,' recalled Flying Officer 'Razz' Berry of No. 603.

There were valid reasons for this solicitude. Those outsiders who saw most of the game—from commanders like Bouchier to flight mechanics like Eric Marsden—realized as no civilian ever could, the strain that The Few were undergoing, the accumulation of fear, fatigue and tension that mounted daily with each scramble.

Although few could have settled for a finite date, the crisis had peaked on July 10, when Professor Frederick Lindemann (later Lord Cherwell), Winston Churchill's scientific advisor, faced with a dearth of trained pilots and a glut of operational machines, had seen no option but to reduce drastically the pilots' operational training—from six months to four weeks. In the belief that the monthly output of pilots could be boosted from 560 to 890, Lindemann had asked: "Are not our standards of training too high? The final polish should be given in the squadrons."

From August 8 onward, as all the participants knew, more and more had acquired 'the final polish', through a cruel baptism of fire. No sooner had many pilots taxied in than they slumped forward in their cockpits, as dead to the world as men under morphia. At Hawkinge, Pilot Officer Peter Hairs, a Hurricane pilot of No. 501 Squadron, was a case in point—"after eight scrambles in a day, you came to write up your log book, and you just couldn't remember, beyond putting down the number of times you'd been up . . . you couldn't remember at all. I had nightmares about blazing planes crashing all around me."

Many soon came to cushion their fears with liquor. Squadron Leader John Worrall of No. 32 Squadron: "If you weren't in the air, you were plastered. It was as simple as that." At the Square Club,

in Andover, where the pilots from Middle Wallop congregated, stupefying mixtures were soon the norm—everything from vocka and apricot brandy to brandy and port. The station medical officer at Warmwell, Middle Wallop's forward base, Flight Lieutenant Monty Bieber, remembered mixing up 'harmless pink drinks' to quieten morning-after stomachs: "It was absolute alcohol, which clinched the hangover effect and gave an excuse to keep them off flying." But one unlucky pilot, Flying Officer Roland Dibnah of No. 1 Squadron, was allergic to liquor. The tension was so great that merely one measure drove Dibnah vomiting to the lavatory.

"I looked up again, and this time I saw them—about a dozen slugs, shining in the bright sun and coming straight on. At the rising scream of the first bomb I instinctively shrugged up my shoulders and ducked my head. Out of the corner of my eye I saw the three Spitfires. One moment they were

page 113: Brian Lane (left) became acting CO of 19 Squadron at Duxford in the Battle of Britain; above left: Crew members of a Heinkel bomber before a mission to England; above right: RAF fighter pilots are delivered to their aircraft in 1940.

about twenty feet up in close formation, the next catapulted apart as though on elastic. The leader went over on his back and ploughed along the runway with a rending crash of tearing fabric; No, 2 put a wing in and spun around on his airscrew, while the plane on the left was blasted wingless into the next field. I remember thinking stupidly, 'That's the shortest flight he's ever taken,' and then my feet were nearly knocked from under me, my mouth was full of dirt, and Bubble gesticulating like a madman from the shelter entrance, was yelling, 'Run, you bloody fool, run!' I ran. Suddenly awakened to the lunacy of my behaviour, I covered the distance to the shelter as if impelled by a rocket and shot through the entrance while once again the ground rose up and hit me, and my head smashed hard against one of the pillars. I subsided on a heap of rubble and massaged it."
—from *The Last Enemy* by Richard Hillary

Every man on the sidelines of the Battle had his own personal yardstick of impending catastrophe. At Tangmere, a thin black line in the mess ledger that recorded each pilot's mealtimes was ruled beneath name after name. Mess steward Joseph Lauderdale, at Middle Wallop, remembered that his pilots often died too soon to qualify for a change of sheets. Aircraftman George Perry, attached to No. 56 Squadron at North Weald, recalled how "boys came back men after an eighty-minute sortie. Faces would be grey. There'd be yellow froth round their mouths."

On August 17, when Fighter Command's thinning ranks were once more stiffened with many Fairey Battle pilots and Army Cooperation Command pilots, the training period was slashed once again—this time from a month to a bare two weeks. On the following day, twenty-seven planes were written off, eighteen pilots were hospitalized and ten pilots embarked on their last scramble.

Yet the steady induction of novices into the firing line only saw the losses mounting. "I'm sorry, but I'm afraid you'll have to go in today," Squadron Leader John Thompson of No. 111 Hurricane Squadron remembered greeting two grass-green sergeants at Debden on August 24, "you see, we're so terribly short." And one of the sergeants, Raymond Sellers, remembered it too; he later awoke in hospital so deeply in shock that even his own name escaped him. Fifteen days earlier, on August 11, he had proudly noted twenty minutes dogfighting practice in his log book.

It is a story that Sellers recounted in humiliation, for his fellow sergeant had died, and at teatime that day the old car they shared was still parked outside the mess with their gear not unpacked, but in truth he was in good company. Ten days later, Flight Lieutenant Al Deere was equally shamefaced when reporting to No. 54 Squadron's intelligence officer, Tony Allen. He had taken bursts at fully six ME 109s, but somehow his bullets had failed to connect. "We're so bloody tired," Deere shrugged it off. "We're just not getting them."

Having this involuntary intimacy with death, men grew increasingly callous, as if to immunize themselves from caring. As Pilot Officer 'Rafty' Rafter's Spitfire spun out of control near Maidstone, Bill Read heard an angry 603 pilot break radio silence: "Bugger—he owed me a fiver!" After hospital treatment, Rafter survived to repay it, but nobody knew that until later. It was the same when Pilot Officer David Bell-Salter was once prematurely written off by the Hurricane pilots of No. 253. A girlfriend of his who called the Kenley mess asking to speak to David was told curtly, "You can't—he's dead," before his pal hung up.

Since a telephone bell denoted a scramble, the fear of bells became a near primal obsession. "I even panicked at bicycle bells," recalled Ronnie Hamlyn, and Bill Read of 603 confirmed, "I was so geared up that even on leave I'd run at the sound of an ambulance bell." Even the ground crews became infected, "For a good ten years after 1940", admitted Eric Marsden, "whenever an electric bell sounded off, I jumped looking for something to do. I was conditioned, like Pavlov's dog!" With Pilot Officer Christopher Currant, of No. 605 Squadron at Croydon, the phobia extended even to running, "If you saw anyone run, you felt you'd got to, too. I hated to see airmen do it. I'd tear strips off them—'Don't run about the place—walk properly.' You got trigger-tense about it."

To pilots coming fresh to the Battle, many of the older hands seemed near to the end of their tether. Even the cheerful Al Deere found his nerves at snapping-point; an unexpected shout over the radio-telephone set his heart pounding like a trip-hammer. Sergeant James 'Ginger' Lacey had to fly with his right foot tucked in the loop of the rudder bar in order to combat the twitching. Pilot Officer Charles Ambrose of No. 46 Hurricane Squadron recalled being genuinely shocked by the lethargy of No. 151

Squadron when they relieved them at Stapleford Tawney on September 1. While 46 had been in reserve at Digby, 151 at North Weald had lost two COs and were down to seven survivors.

The seven were lunching at 11 a.m., Ambrose remembered, when a breathless telephone orderly announced the controller's scramble order. He remembered too, their flight commander's withering reply: "Tell him we're finishing our bloody lunch first."

Wing Commander Geoffrey Page remembered being shot down on August 12: "The first bang came as a shock. For an instant I couldn't believe I'd been hit. Two more bangs followed in quick succession, and as if by magic, a gaping hole suddenly appeared in my starboard wing.

"Surprise quickly changed to fear, and as the instinct of self-preservation began to take over, the gas tank behind the engine blew up, and my cockpit became an inferno. Fear became blind terror, then agonizing horror as the bare skin of my hands gripping the throttle and control column shrivelled up like burnt parchment under the intensity of the blast furnace temperature.

Messerschmitt Bf 110 day/night fighters on a French airfield in 1940.

"Screaming at the top of my voice, I threw my head back to keep it away from the searing flames. Instinctively the tortured right hand groped for the release pin securing the restraining Sutton harness.

"Dear God, save me, dear God . . . I cried imploringly. Then, as suddenly as terror had overtaken me, it vanished with the knowledge that death was no longer to be feared. My fingers kept up their blind and bloody mechanical groping. Some large mechanical dark object disappeared between my legs and cool, relieving fresh air suddenly flowed across my burning face. I tumbled. Sky, sea, sky, over and over as a clearing brain issued instructions to outflung limbs. 'Pull the ripcord—right hand to the ripcord. Watering eyes focused on an arm flung out in space with some strange meaty object attached at its end.

"More tumbling—more sky and sea and sky, but with a blue-clad arm forming a focal point in the foreground. 'Pull the ripcord, hand,' the brain again commanded. Slowly but obediently the elbow bent and the hand came across the body to rest on the chromium ring but bounced away quickly with the agony of contact.

"More tumbling but at a slower rate now. The weight of the head was beginning to tell.

"Realizing that pain or no pain, the ripcord had to be pulled, the brain overcame the reaction of the raw nerve endings and forced the mutilated fingers to grasp the ring and pull firmly.

"It acted immediately. With a jerk the silken canopy billowed out in the clear summer sky. It was then that I noticed the smell. The odor of my burnt flesh was so loathsome that I wanted to vomit. But there was too much to attend to, even for that small luxury. Self-preservation was my first concern, and my chance for it looked slim. The coastline at Margate was just discernable six to ten miles away. Ten thousand feet below me lay the deserted sea. Not a ship or a seagull crossed its blank, grey surface.

"Still looking down I began to laugh. The force of the exploding gas tank had blown every vestige of clothing off from my thighs downwards, including one shoe. Carefully I eased off the remaining shoe with the toes of the other foot and watched the tumbling footwear in the hope of seeing it strike the water far beneath. Now came the bad time.

"The shock of my violent injuries was starting to take hold, and this combined with the cold air at the high altitude brought on a shivering attack that was quite uncontrollable. With that, the parachute began to sway, setting up a violent oscillating movement with my teeth-chattering torso acting as a human pendulum. Besides its swinging movement it began a gentle turn and shortly afterwards the friendly shoreline disappeared behind my back. This brought with it an *idée fixe* that if survival was to be achieved, then the coast must be kept in sight. A combination of agonized curses and bleeding hands pulling on the shrouds finally brought about the desired effect, and I settled back to the pleasures of closing eyes and burnt flesh.

"Looking down again I was surprised to find that the water had come up to meet me very rapidly since last I had taken stock. This called for some fairly swift action if the parachute was to be discarded a second or two before entering the water. The procedure itself was quite simple. Lying over my stomach was a small metal release box which clasped the four ends of the parachute harness after they had passed down over the shoulders and up from the groin. On this box was a circular metal disc which had to be turned through ninety degrees, banged, and presto! The occupant was released from the 'chute. All of this was extremely simple except in the case of fingers which refused to turn the little disc.

Captive German bomber crewmen whose aircraft was downed over England in the Blitz.

"The struggle was still in progress when I plunged feet first in the water. Despite the beauties of the summer and the wealth of warm days that had occurred, the sea felt icy cold to my badly shocked body. Kicking madly, I came to the surface to find my arms entangled with the multiple shrouds holding me in an octopus-like grip. The battle with the metal disc still had to be won, or else the water-logged parachute would eventually drag me down to a watery grave. Spluttering with mouthfuls of salt water I struggled grimly with the vital release mechanism. Pieces of flesh flaked off and blood poured from the raw tissues.

"Desperation, egged on by near panic, forced the decision, and with a sob of relief I found that the disc had surrendered the battle.

"Kicking away blindly at the tentacles that still entwined arms and legs, I fought free and swam fiercely away from the nightmare surroundings of the parachute. Wild fear died away and the simple rules of procedure for continued existence exerted themselves again.

"'Get rid of the 'chute and then inflate your Mae West,' said the book of rules, and 'float about until rescued.'

"'That's all very well,' I thought, 'but unless I get near to the coast under my own steam, there's not much chance of being picked up.' With that I trod water and extricated the long rubber tube with which to blow up the jacket. Unscrewing the valves between my teeth, I searched my panting lungs for extra air. The only result after several minutes of exertion was a feeling of dizzyness and a string

below: A Hurricane fighter at the Westhampnett satellite of Tangmere; right: A Bf 109 shot down over England in 1940.

of bubbles from the bottom of the jacket. The fire had burnt a large hole through the rubber bladder.

"Dismay was soon replaced by fatalism. There was the distant shore, unseen but positioned by reference to the sun, and only one method of getting there, so it appeared. Turning on my stomach I set out at a measured stroke. Ten minutes of acute misery passed by as the salt dried about my face injuries and the contracting strap of the flying helmet cut into the raw surface of my chin. Buckle and leather had welded into one solid mass, preventing removal of the headgear.

"Dumb despair then suddenly gave way to shining hope. The brandy flask, of course. This was it—the emergency for which it was kept. But the problem of undoing the tunic remained, not to mention that the tight-fitting Mae West covered the pocket as another formidable barrier. Hope and joy were running too high to be deterred by such mundane problems, and so turning with my face to the sky I set about the task of getting slightly tipsy on neat brandy. Inch by inch my ultra-sensitive fingers worked their way under the Mae West towards the breast pocket. Every movement brought with it indescribable agony, but the goal was too great to allow for weakness. At last the restraining copper button was reached—a deep breath to cope with all the pain—and it was undone.

"Automatically my legs kept up their propulsive efforts while my hand had a rest from its labours. Then gingerly the flask was eased out of its home and brought to the surface of the water. Pain became conqueror for a while and the flask was transferred to a position between my wrists. Placing the screw stopper between my teeth, I undid it with a series of head-twists and finally the great

moment arrived—the life-warming liquid was waiting to be drunk. Raising it to my mouth, I pursed my lips to drink. The flask slipped from between wet wrists and disappeared from sight. Genuine tears of rage followed this newest form of torture, which in turn gave place to a furious determination to swim to safety.

"After the first few angry strokes despair returned in full force, ably assisted by growing fatigue, cold and pain. Time went by unregistered. Was it minutes, hours or days since my flaming Hurricane disappeared between my legs? Was it getting dark or were my eyes closing up? How could I steer towards the shore if I couldn't see the sun? How could I see the sun if that rising pall of smoke obscured it from sight?

"That rising pall of smoke … that rising pall of smoke. No, it couldn't be. I yelled. I splashed the water with my arms and legs until the pain brought me to a sobbing halt. Yes, the smoke was coming from a funnel—but supposing it passed without seeing me? Agony of mind was greater than agony of body and the shouting and splashing recommenced. Looking again, almost expecting that smoke and funnel had been an hallucination, I gave a fervent gasp of thanks to see that whatever ship it was, it had hove to.

"All of the problems were fast disappearing and only one remained. It was one of keeping afloat for just another minute or two before all energy failed. Then I heard it—the unmistakalbe chug-chug of a small motor boat growing louder and louder. Soon it came into sight with a small bow wave pouring away to each side. In it sat two men in the strange garb peculiar to sailors of the British Merchant Service. The high-revving note of the engine died to a steady throb as the man astride the engine throttled back. A rough voice carried over the intervening water. 'What are you, a Jerry or one of ours?'

"My weak reply was gagged by a mouthful of water. The other man tried as the boat came full circle for the second time. 'Are you a Jerry, mate?'

"Anger flooded through me. Anger, not at these sailors who had every reason to let a German pilot drown, but anger at the steady chain of events since the explosion that had reduced my tortured mind and body to its present state of near-collapse. And anger brought with it temporary energy. 'You stupid pair of bastards! Pull me out!

"The boat altered course and drew alongside. Strong arms leaned down and dragged my limp body over the side and into the bottom of the boat. 'The minute you swore, mate,' one of them explained, 'we knew you was an RAF officer.'

The sodden, dripping bundle was deposited on a wooden seat athwart ships. A voice mumbled from an almost lifeless body as the charred helmet was removed. One of the sailors leaned down to catch the words. 'What did you say, chum?' The mumble was more distinct for the second time. 'Take me to the side. I want to be sick.'

"The other man answered in a friendly voice, 'You do it in the bottom of the boat and we'll clean up afterwards.'

"But habit died hard and pride wouldn't permit it, so keeping my head down between my knees, I was able to control the sensation of nausea. Allowing me a moment or two to feel better, the first sailor produced a large clasp knife. 'Better get this wet stuff off you, mate. You don't want to catch your death of cold.'

"The absurdity of death from a chill struck me as funny and I chuckled for the first time in a long

Bomb damage in Portsmouth,
1940.

while. To prove the sailor's point, the teeth-chattering recommenced. Without further ado the man with the knife set to work and deftly removed pieces of life jacket and tunic with the skill of a surgeon. Then my naked body was wrapped up in a blanket produced from the seat locker.

"One of them went forward to the engine and seconds later the little boat was churning her way back to the mother ship. The other sailor sat down beside me in silence, anxious to help but not knowing what to do next. I sensed the kindness of his attitude and felt that it was up to me to somehow offer him a lead. The feeling of sickness was still there from the revolting smell of burnt flesh, but I managed to gulp out 'Been a lovely summer . . . hasn't it?'

"The man nodded. 'Aye.'"

left: RAF fighter pilot Sergeant G. A. Whipps of 602 Squadron, Westhampnett in September 1940; below: Heavy bomb damage in the area surrounding St Paul's cathedral, London, in 1941.

A fine study of Heinkel He 111
bombers crossing the English Channel in
a raid on a British target during the Blitz.

PICTURE CREDITS: ALL PHOTOGRAPHS FROM THE COLLECTION OF THE AUTHOR ARE CREDITED AC. P3 LEFT-AC, RIGHT-DAVID LOW; P4 ALL-AC; P5-AC; PP6-7 ALL-VICKERS; P8 BOTH-VICKERS; P9-VICKERS; P10 ALL-AC; P11-AC; P13-AC; P14 ALL-AC; P15-AC; P16 TOP-AC, BOTTOM-A. SAUNDERS; P19 ALL-AC; P20 ALL-AC; P21-AC; PP22-23-AC; P24 ALL-AC; P27 TOP LEFT-A. SAUNDERS, TOP RIGHT AND BOTTOM-AC; PP28-29-M. O'LEARY; P31 ALL-AC; P32 ALL-AC; P35 ALL-AC; P37-AC; PP38-39 ALL-C. ORDE; PP40-41 ALL-C. ORDE; P42-AC; P44-AC; P46 BOTTOM-A. SAUNDERS, TOP BOTH-AC; P47 ALL-AC; P48 ALL-AC; P49-BUNDESARCHIV; P50-BUNDESARCHIV; P51-BOTH BUNDESARCHIV; P53 TOP-BUNDESARCHIV, BOTTOM-AC; PP54-55-AC; P56 TOP-AC, BOTTOM-RAF MUSEUM; P57 BOTH-AC; P59 BOTH-AC; P61 BOTH-AC; PP62-63 ALL-AC; PP64-65 ALL-AC; P66-AC; P68 TOP-BUNDESARCHIV, BOTTOM-AC; P69-BUNDESARCHIV; P71 TOP AND BOTTOM LEFT-AC, BOTTOM RIGHT-E. KUP; P72-AC; P74-AC; P75-BUNDESARCHIV; P76-E. MARSDEN; P77-BUNDESARCHIV; P78 ALL-AC; P79-A. SAUNDERS; PP80-81-AC; P83 BOTH-AC; P84-IMPERIAL WAR MUSEUM; P85-BUNDESARCHIV; P87 BOTH-AC; P89-BUNDESARCHIV; P90-A. SAUNDERS; P91-BUNDESARCHIV; P92-BUNDESARCHIV; P93-AC; P94-M. AGAZARIAN; P95 BOTH-D.B. WALKER; P96-AC; P97 BOTH-AC; P98-RAF MUSUEM; P99-AC; P101-AC; P102-A. SAUNDERS; P103-AC; PP104-105-AC; P107-AC; PP108-109-AC; P110-J. BURGESS; P113-RAF MUSEUM; P114-BUNDESARCHIV; P115-AC; P117-AC; P119-AC; P120-E. MARSDEN; P121-A. SAUNDERS; P123-AC; P124-A.SAUNDERS; P125-AC; PP126-127-BUNDESARCHIV; P128-AC.